Born Again
...but still wet
behind the ears

Born Again ...but still wet behind the ears

ANN KINDIG SHEETZ

CHRISTIAN HERALD BOOKS
Chappaqua, New York

Copyright © 1979 by Ann Kindig Sheetz

Library of Congress Cataloging in Publication Data

Sheetz, Ann Kindig.
  Born again, but still wet behind the ears.

  1. Sheetz, Ann Kindig.   2. Christian biography—
United States.   3. Christian life—1960-   I. Title.
BR1725.S454A33   248'.2[B]   78-684839
ISBN 0-915684-43-8

First Edition

CHRISTIAN HERALD BOOKS, 40 Overlook Drive, Chappaqua, New York 10514

Printed in the United States of America

To
Loren, Todd, Doug,
Mom and Dad

Introduction

Many years ago a family lived in a log cabin in the corner of what is now our yard. It was a large, close-knit clan and as each child married the father built a cabin for the newlyweds. Soon many little houses dotted the area. It became known as Pucky Huddle, a community not to be found on any map nor preserved in history books but one that was complete with store and a one-room school just up the road.

In time, the houses of Pucky Huddle were vacated and one by one torn down or burned. The original cabin was dismantled sometime after the turn of the century when our house was built. Logs from it were used as sills in a machine shed, all that remains of the settlement, unless you count horseweeds with stalks as thick as a child's arm that grow so tall a man standing on a tractor cannot see over them or thistles as sharp as any acupuncture kit that thrive in spite of our constant attempts to eradicate them.

We have lived in Pucky Huddle more than twenty-two years, fighting a losing battle with the primeval jungle that must have choked the little village to death, yet loving it enough to preserve the name with a sign that boasts: Pucky Huddle —Pop. 4.

Pucky Huddle is our refuge, our place to restore, but it is only part of our lives. The rest of our time, the biggest share of it, in fact, is caught up in the deadlines of publishing a weekly newspaper.

It's a strange combination—farming and news-papering—and ours is a way of life both simple and complicated, one in which we cast many footprints, not a few of which are in the wind.

Still, it is a way of life filled with joy and laughter too great to keep to ourselves and for the past twelve years I've shared it with our readers through a weekly column called "Odds and Ends," although a more appropriate title might be "Confessions of a Closet Christian." Our lives constantly guided by God, we've come to view prayer as necessary as food itself, but we've tended to take too literally Christ's admonition that when we pray we should go into our closet, shut the door and pray to our Father in secret. Too often, we've stayed in the closet, keeping our faith itself a secret.

When Jesus said, "Take up your cross and follow me," he didn't say the way would be easy, that it wouldn't be strewn with stumbling blocks. Some of these—our habits, customs and past experiences, to name but a few—make it all too easy for many of us to hide in our closets, afraid to reveal too much of ourselves. In today's idiom, we may have been born again, but we've still got a lot of growing up to do.

Then, too, some of us witness more easily than others. I don't do it well because of a flaw in my makeup. A friend describes it as "having your kidneys too close to your eyes." Translated, that means I'm a weeper, easily moved by beautiful music, babies, flowers, sunsets, acts of love, the witness of others. And while I've come to understand my tears are a testimony, I stubbornly prefer to witness without having to dab my eyes or blow my nose. "God, you've been so good to us," I used to pray. "Help me share this joy." Then, as if anticipating the answer, I'd retreat into my closet, slamming shut the door of true Christianity by adding, "Just don't expect me to witness. You know I'd make a mess of it."

8

It was a long time before I realized that the columns are my way of witnessing, that God answered my prayers in spite of my qualifying statement. Sometimes it appears I acknowledge God merely as a sprig of parsley, a garnish, if at all, but I know nothing could be further from the truth. My family's love of God penetrates these columns as surely as it provides the tie that binds our love for each other, for the good earth that sustains us, for the smell and feel of printer's ink that long ago permeated our veins. It's our link to a segment of Americana not yet completely taken over by computers and burglar alarm systems, one where neighbors bring cookies if we're sick, sit with our children if we're busy, or just stop by to visit.

This rewriting of those columns is our life, and we welcome you to it with a few words of warning: You will not read any advice about finding God in the hay mow or under a typesetter. Nor will you find a chronological report of what each of our children did in his first, second or nineteenth year. And certainly no flowery words of wisdom on rearing children. A few chuckles, a few tears, but not much advice.

But you will find I'm no longer a closet Christian. The door did open, very slowly and very painfully. And it didn't reveal a saint with all her theologies in good order, but a faltering, born-again Christian still very wet behind the ears, ready at last to take up the cross and follow.

And you will find, too, a realization that the way, while not always easy and often strewn with stumbling blocks of our own making, is not without humor. That too is reflected, I trust, in the book's title. Not all laughter and easy living—no one said love, marriage, family, home and job would be any simpler to harness than our footprints as they swirl in the wind—but certainly not without cause for celebration and supplication. That realization is what this book is all about.

CHAPTER ONE

Best of Two Worlds

The guys in green and gold were ours; the ones in blue were the opponents. Armed with that bit of knowledge and a camera, I went to the second football game of my life. All I could remember of the first—had it really been twenty-five years ago?—was the cute drum major whose autograph I got. I had a dim recollection, too, of a photographer dashing up and down the sidelines trying for action pictures.

Now I was that reporter, sent off to the gridiron by my devoted family with the calm assurance, "You'll do fine."

The game was in progress when I arrived. The scoreboard showed our guys were ahead. I watched as they ran east. Then they ran west. Sometimes the fellows in blue ran after them; sometimes they chased them. When they weren't chasing each other, they got together in gossipy huddles and then lined up facing the other team with one boy throwing the ball between his legs to someone on his team.

I didn't understand it, but I did know that sooner or later someone would try to make a touchdown. "Which goal post is ours?" I whispered to a friend. She gave me a funny look and motioned to the west one.

I refocused my camera, muttering to myself, "If I could just see the ball, I'd be happy." And then it happened. One of our guys ran past me with the ball under his arm, and I snapped a picture as he ran off the field. The fans went wild.

He hadn't run between the goal posts so I figured it didn't count, but someone slapped me on the shoulder and yelled, "It's a touchdown!" Then one of the boys tried to kick the ball between the goal posts. It was the only time I ever saw a foot connect with the ball, and I wondered how the game got its name.

I'd taken pictures of our guys the night before and had been impressed with their friendliness and politeness. I couldn't recognize them now in their helmets, but they looked like the same fellows I'd seen run and jump and do calisthenics. I watched them with something akin to motherly pride, and when one of them jumped at a boy in blue who had the ball, I cringed. Nice boys don't act like bullies just because they don't have a ball. I'd been to enough basketball games to know that would be a charging foul, and I waited to see what happened. The fans shrieked. "Atta way to go!" a voice shouted as someone screamed in my ear, "That kid's going to be a great tackle!"

And so it went. Back and forth, back and forth, now at the blue, now away from them. Sometimes the umpire threw red scarves in the air and everyone watched to see where they landed. It was a great way to spend a morning. I took pictures of everything, visiting with friends as I ran up and down the field.

"How'd it go?" my family asked when I returned.

I told them.

The boys just stared at me. For once they were speechless.

Loren didn't say much, but he shook a lot. Finally, he dabbed his eyes and asked, "Would you like to be a full-time sports reporter?"

"Okay, laugh," I growled. "I may not know much about football, but I *can* take pictures. I even got one of a touchdown run." They were impressed.

But when they developed the film, I saw the horrible

truth: the boy not only ran off the field, he also ran out of the camera's range. The only good picture I had was one of the scarf. (And they told me it's called a flag.)

I threatened to put the picture with the drum major's autograph and learn to tat, but I knew I couldn't. When you're the only reporter, you have to be adaptable, especially if you're also editor, bookkeeper, ad salesperson, secretary and janitor.

And you don't take time to ask how you got into situations like that. You know. In my case, it had to do with a lifetime dream that came true and a plan Loren and I brought home from Germany when we were twenty-three and twenty-four and Todd, our first-born, was six months old. It was a time of readjustment, of planning a more stable lifestyle now that the military service we'd expected since we were married was finally over.

The plan came first. "Theirs shall be the best of two worlds," we said. "Our children will know the joys of both rural and urban life."

We knew God had helped our five-year-old teen-age marriage confound statisticians who had given it not more than two, and we prayed he would help us rear our children as we had been—on a farm. Life on the economy of a large German city had convinced us there is a lot of truth to the old saying that you can take the boy out of the country but you can't take the country out of the boy. (Or girl.) But traveling had been fun, and we had enjoyed much that city living had to offer. We saw no reason the two lifestyles could not blend into one when we decided to live in the country and work in town. Todd and the girl we would add later would be able to revel in the glories of God that seem so abundant in the country, yet be free to stay after school for plays, clubs, sports or Coke dates.

We moved to a thirty-acre farm that we named Pucky

Huddle after the village that once dotted its fields and turned an empty peanut butter jar into a Germany bank that would finance future trips. Within a few years, my lifetime dream of owning a weekly newspaper was realized, and we knew God had spoken. There was no reason our best of two worlds plan should fail.

"The best of two worlds." The words had a happy sound.

Such were our dreams. But, as surely as our daughter was a second son, Doug, they have not followed the pattern we planned. That they are succeeding at all is proof of God's infinite goodness even to those of us who fail to thoroughly investigate the course we think is right for us. Closer inspection of our "two worlds" would have revealed that a town of less than one thousand is not a city, that a weekly newspaper is more than rumpled tweeds and cluttered roll-tops and that thirty acres cannot support a family. Our two worlds are really one — a rural way of life threatened by corporate farms, suburban shopping centers and mass media.

But the boys don't care that time is too scarce to travel, that the Germany bank has never contained enough money for the four of us to eat in a German restaurant, much less buy airline tickets. Neither do they care for our best of two worlds attitude, because they have almost totally rejected one in favor of the other. There will be no taking the boy out of the country for them; they do not intend to leave. They prefer hauling manure, baling hay, raising hogs — anything that sounds even vaguely farm-related — to learning the intricacies of printing. They will work in the darkroom if it is raining and farm work is temporarily halted, but they abhor cleaning. It interferes with farming. Actually setting type, which is now child's play in comparison with the hot method we employed when we bought the paper, is considered cruelty to children.

As for staying after school, that's boring. It's more fun to

13

ride the bus home, even if they spend the next two hours watching television.

Doug summed up their feelings when he said, "I don't know why you and Dad don't get into something sensible instead of putting out a newspaper — something like farming."

And so we travel little. We have to coerce the boys to help at the office, and meal schedules are set by harvests and planting. But I suppose in the end it is their father and I who have won, for they truly have the best of both worlds: they eat from the fruits of our labors in one and glory in the freedom of the other.

God truly answered our prayers in giving us the opportunity to live in the best of two worlds. But like his call to us to come out of our closets, he didn't say the way would be easy, and it's only when I have to cover football games or sort the laundry — ink stains in one pile, manure and hay in the other — that I know who got the worst of both worlds.

CHAPTER TWO

Love and Marriage

Spin the Chair

Years ago, we played "spin the milk bottle." Apparently the spinning motion was appealing, because for most of our marriage Loren and I have played a more grown-up version called "spin the rocking chair."

We don't touch those chairs in the living room or den that swivel or rock. We concentrate all our energies on a sturdy, hard-as-granite rocker in the dining room.

Located as it is between two windows and next to the kitchen, it affords me a quiet place to meditate or read while I listen for potatoes to boil or wait for a cake to finish baking. Or I can watch the ditch bank where I once saw a mother skunk leading her pack of babies nose-to-tail-nose-to-tail or the neighbor's woods where sometimes the morning sun suspends brilliant silver crosses in the sycamores.

It's the same rocking chair that, if turned ninety degrees, lets Loren read while I prepare a meal or lets him watch the wind sock, his weather instruments or the creek where we sometimes see deer.

My way looks forward; his turns the chair's back to the room. He finds his way appealing; I find it confining. I like to see the road; he turns from it to the yard and fields. His way disrupts my sense of order; a chair should not turn its back to a room. My way threatens his world.

And so we spin. Before I go to bed, I set things right. The

chair turns. As soon as he gets up, he writes in his weather diary and the chair turns again. Before I go to work, I turn the chair. Come evening, he "keeps me company" while I get supper by turning the chair to the window and using the sill for a footstool.

The chair is seldom actually used, but it moves a lot. Even the boys have begun to notice.

"Gee, they sure don't agree much, do they?" Doug observed. "Wonder how they ever got together in the first place?"

"I'm not sure," Todd replied, "but I think it was some kind of lottery. I heard Dad tell someone he won her playing 'spin the milk bottle.' "

Conventional

"You're a lot more conventional than I am," Loren argued.

"Me!" I exploded. "How do you figure? Anyone who wears only black pants and socks has got to be pretty conventional."

"Pretty unconventional, you mean," he said. "Everyone else wears a lot of colors. Not me. Any shirt will go with any pair of pants. I don't have to stand around wondering what color shirt and socks I'm allowed with turquoise pants."

"And you're the guy who said I was an old maid when I refused to wear short skirts," I countered.

"You look better in them."

"My legs are too fat."

"That just shows how conventional you are. If you weren't conventional, you wouldn't worry about weight."

Would you believe the debate started when I told him Frank and Lucy, children of friends of ours, were going to hitchhike through Europe? He said, "Why can't kids do something conventional for a change?" and I said, "It'd be a shame if everyone followed the same conventions. Just because everyone else does something doesn't mean we

16

have to do the same thing." And he said, "The only way to get ahead in the world is by being conventional." The next thing we knew, we were each trying to out-unconventional the other.

Hearing the racket, the boys stuck their heads in the door and watched silently while I suggested anyone who always bought six-cylinder cars and trucks was uncompromisingly conventional, and he told me he was the unconventional one because he just happened to prefer six over eight, no matter what everyone else did.

"Wow! How do you suppose that got started?" Doug asked.

"They're just being conventional," Todd replied. "It's standard procedure for parents. If we wanted to hitchhike through Europe, she'd tell us we were crazy and to stick with something more conventional."

"I heard that," I snapped. "You guys get out of here. Your conventional father and I are having a discussion."

"Who's conventional?" Loren demanded.

"I don't even know what it means," Doug said.

"You should. Look at those blue jeans," his father said. "You're as conventional as they come, always wearing blue jeans. Why don't you wear some of your other pants?"

"Because I like blue jeans," the boy protested. "They go with everything."

"A little variety never hurt anyone," Loren said.

"Could I vary my way of getting to school today by driving?" Todd asked.

"No way," Loren and I replied in unison.

"Now, where were we?" Loren asked as the boys left.

"I don't know. Some sort of discussion about which of us is the more conventional. Or unconventional."

"Well, I think. . .," he started, his sentence trailing off as we heard the voices from the other room.

"So what is conventional?" Doug asked.

17

"Mom and Dad," Todd replied. "If they do it, it's unconventional. If everyone else does it, it's conventional. Doesn't matter if they're ahead of or behind the times. Their whole attitude is conventional."

"You mean like us having to take showers and brush our teeth?"

"Yeah, and going to bed on time and their going to work every day."

"It doesn't sound like much fun."

"It isn't. That's why they're arguing. When you're conventional, that's all you can do for fun."

Impending Disaster

It was a Saturday evening so typical it could have been duplicated in fifty thousand living rooms across the country. Husband slouched in his chair, half asleep, paper half on, half off his stomach. Two boys glued to television. Mother making dozens of trips past as she carries mounds of clean clothes upstairs.

Only this Saturday was different and on my thirteenth lap, I kicked Loren's foot to wake him. When he blinked, I demanded, "Do you know what anniversary this is?"

He thought a bit, tugged at his paper, and shrugged. "I don't know. What?"

"Of the day you gave me my engagement ring," I said, martyr-like, as I refolded the boys' underwear.

"Gee," he said, "how'd you happen to remember a thing like that?"

I could have reminded him of the promises he made that night or even of the dunking in the shower I got when I returned to the dormitory or the all-night gab session with my friends. Instead, I shifted my load and said, "Association, I guess. I always remember it was the day before the anniversary of Pearl Harbor."

"Hmpf," he said, pulling the paper over his head, this man who had promised to swim the deepest river and climb the highest mountain for me. "Sort of like a warning of impending disaster, huh?"

He fell asleep so quickly he didn't notice when I threw a stack of socks at him. For once, the boys said nothing. They were watching television and, besides, they had never heard of Pearl Harbor.

Poker Game

"Get the president's autograph," I said.

"Just get me anything," Doug suggested.

It was senior trip time, and we were advising Todd, who was clearly bored by it all.

"Stay out of poker games," Loren said.

I glared at him, but both boys were immediately interested.

"Poker games?" Todd asked. "On a senior trip?"

"Poker games."

"Just have fun," I said, but it was too late to tell him about our own senior trip, a much longer affair than the one-day fling these seniors would make to Washington. Too late to tell him of the long train ride to Washington and later to New York, because already he was watching his father intently.

"Some people on our trip got pretty lucky at poker," Loren said, looking at me and grinning.

The boys jumped at the chance to "get Mom."

"What happened?" Doug asked.

"Not much," I answered. "Some of the kids taught the rest of us to play poker. That's all."

"Yeah, and 'some' of us did okay," Loren replied.

"Well, I made enough to buy a couple sandwiches," I conceded.

19

"What are you driving at?" Todd asked his father. "What else did she win?"

"Me."

"She won you in a poker game? How'd she do that?"

"She got everything else I had; I was the only thing left."

"That's crazy," Todd said, but Doug thought the odds sounded pretty good.

"Boy, you sure set him up," I told Loren the next morning as we heard Todd leave.

"Might as well learn the truth sometime," he muttered, rolling over and going back to sleep while I lay awake, alternately thanking God for a marriage secure enough to permit teasing and wondering why we tell our kids such preposterous yarns.

We thought about the seniors all day, wondering how they liked Washington, what ours would have to report.

"How was your trip?" I asked our bleary-eyed son when he returned late that night.

"Real good."

"What'd you learn?" his father asked.

"You know," Todd said, "you'd have to be awfully dumb to lose yourself in a poker game."

"Is that what you learned?" his startled father asked. But he was too late. The traveler had already headed for shower and bed.

"Wonder what he did learn?" he asked.

"Dunno," I mumbled. It was my turn to sleep while he lay awake and worried.

Gimme a Hundred Good Reasons

The day was dark and dreary, and the downpour did nothing for anyone's morale. Everything Loren had planned to do over the weekend had been rained out and now, as a new week began, his truck wouldn't start. He fumed, fussed and fiddled with it. He tinkered with it while I operated the starter. Nothing happened. He climbed back in the cab, water streaming from his nose and ears and trickling off his hair, to give it "one more chance." It started, but it was too late. He was in a foul mood and growled, "With the week starting like this, everything is bound to go wrong. It's an awful day."

I hadn't reached the same degree of wateritis, and I said cheerfully, "I think it's a wonderful day!"

"Gimme a hundred good reasons why it is," he countered as he set off to sell advertising. I promised to hand him a list at noon.

Doing the office work with my hands, I found my thoughts occupied with the list as I noted that Todd was almost recovered from a bout with infected tonsils, Doug was well, we had had neither eggs nor cereal for breakfast and the furnace and pump were both working. I added that the car had started right away and that even the truck had eventually started. Throwing in his family's love and his faith in God, I itemized who in the family was feeling better than he had a year or two years ago and the fact that the milk hadn't been sour that morning. (With two boys around, it doesn't last long enough to sour, but it looked impressive on the list.)

After about fifty reasons, the list slowed until I remembered his watch was still running after twelve years of faithful service, the water softener hadn't broken down for several weeks and no irate subscribers had called before breakfast. The list was completed in time, and his mood changed considerably after he read it. In fact, he laughed harder than he had since I'd changed hairstyles.

"Everyone should do that once in awhile," I said that evening at supper.

He nodded agreement. "Get out the list. I want to add something."

"What?" I asked softly, hoping for a compliment, as I

21

watched him write, "Thank God we don't have eggplant every night."

Bolts in the Jello

Every time Loren says, "There's a conspiracy against me," I shudder, because I know what has happened. He's bit into another nut, another piece of egg shell, a bone or possibly even a bolt.

"If at first you don't succeed, you're running about average," has become his motto. He has yet to succeed in getting something — anything — without finding something else in it.

If we have eggs, his invariably has a microscopic bit of shell I overlooked. If I make cookies or buy them, it doesn't matter, his has a bit of nut shell. If it's chicken and noodles, you know who finds a bone. And he's the only member of the family who can find a stone in the soup beans, a bone in shrimp or even a pearl in an oyster.

He probably would blame me for the crunchy situation if he didn't have the same thing happen in other places — such as the time we went to a fund-raising dinner and he was the only one of hundreds present who found a bolt in his Jello. It was a huge thing. No one knew how it got there, but we knew who it was intended for.

"You just have a magnetic personality," I told him as we drove home.

"Why can't someone else have a magnetic personality just once?" he muttered, rubbing his aching jaw and counting his teeth with his tongue. "Why is it always me?"

"God endowed each of us with different talents. Yours is special."

"God didn't plan for me to bite bolts," he replied. "He didn't say life would be a bowl of Jello, but he didn't intend me to eat bolts and egg shells and bones."

"Trade you," I offered the last time we had chicken salad. It didn't work. His still was the portion with the bone in it.

When the boys decided they wanted to buy a metal detector, I refused. "Nothing doing," I said. "Just use your father. With his ability, he's bound to find it for you."

Strange Bedfellows

"Now what are you doing?" Loren asked.

"Putting on socks."

"Knee socks? In bed?"

"Yes, in bed. It's cold."

He eyed my outfit — a long flannel nightgown pulled over pajamas that didn't quite cover the socks. "Why don't you get in bed and quit jumping up and down? You'll wear out your socks."

I counted the layers of blankets and added another for good measure. Loren rolled his eyes heavenward and gasped, "I'll suffocate before morning. I can't even move."

"It's 21 below zero outside," I reminded him as I eased between the blankets.

His side of the bed radiated heat and he said, "If you promise not to tickle me with those fuzzy socks, back up and I'll let you warm your feet on mine."

I know now what Ecclesiastes means when it says, "If two lie together, then they have heat, but how can one alone be warm?" But I wonder why men were born warm and women cold. I've spent a lifetime backing up to registers, radiators, oven doors, my husband, anywhere there is a bit of heat. I continued to shiver while Loren dropped into a comfortable sleep and I moved back to my side of the bed.

"Warm already?" he asked sleepily.

"You were snoring on my back. Your breath is cold."

"Oh, for heaven's sake, just lie still. This bed is warm as toast."

23

"It's 21 below outside. There's a 30-mile-per-hour wind. You know it's cold."

"All I know is if you had any more blankets on this bed we could cook breakfast right here."

By morning, he had tossed most of the covers off his side of the bed and I'd taken them to mine. Wrapped like a cocoon, I huddled in a snug, fetal-like position, dreading to get up, plotting my course from bed to dresser to closet and downstairs. Or should I run downstairs and start breakfast before going to the dresser? The decision took another fifteen minutes and by then it was almost time for the school bus. I forced myself into the cold world, grateful only that we had no farrowing sows, laboring cows or newborn lambs to demand our attention in the barn.

It was only after the bus had been met and we were relaxing over second cups of tea and coffee that I noticed Loren's faraway expression.

"A penny for your thoughts?"

"I was just thinking if politics makes strange bedfellows, cold weather makes lots stranger ones."

"You're just jealous because you don't have knee socks," I said as I searched for boots and coats and scarves and gloves and plotted my route from the house to the garage, praying for strength to get past the first door.

Because of You

As soon as I found the card, I knew it was perfect for Loren. "Happy Father's Day to my husband who is celebrating the day . . . because of me."

"Perfect," I chuckled. "Absolutely right."

"Pretty cute," he said when he opened it. "Right, too," he added, laughing.

"Hey, Dad," Doug said, bursting into the room before I

could add any of the choice innuendoes husbands and wives reserve for each other on such occasions. "Let's get that fence fixed before the calves get out again."

"Okay," Loren said tiredly, following our twelve-year-old to the garage for barbed wire and nails, but not before he'd muttered over his shoulder, "Because of you."

"Hey, Dad, can you help me with the battery charger? Todd asked later as the fence builders returned to the garage. "Because of you," Loren shouted, cupping his hands to form a megaphone to direct the sound to the house.

And when the telephone rang and it was for one of the boys, he yelled, "Because of you," as he went in search of the person being called. And he said it later when the belt slipped off the lawnmower and when the truck had to be emptied so a bicycle could be loaded and when he was reminded it had been some time since he had gone fishing with his younger son or had helped work on any of the older boy's vehicles.

"Happy Father's Day," I said as he finally settled into his recliner for his Sunday afternoon nap.

"Because of you . . ." he said, his voice trailing off in a snore.

Next year, I may get him a plain sheet of paper on which he can write his own message. Then if it doesn't turn out right I can give him a wicked grin and say sweetly, "It's all because of you."

It's sad that we wives and husbands can't really communicate our joy *with* each other *to* each other. Being loved and cherished until death do us part is the backbone of marriage, the strength and stability that separate it from "meaningful relationships."

So why is it so hard to tell our mates how we feel about them? Like my witnessing, I suppose tears are part of the

25

reason. I can't express truly deep feelings without crying. Loren can't watch me dab my eyes without teasing me, although I know he's moved too.

Instead, we blunder along, clutching to our hearts memory pictures that were never actually snapped for family scrapbooks. Pictures of us when we exchanged wedding vows and traded rings to show the world we belonged to each other. Only his ring wouldn't go over his knuckle no matter how hard I pushed, and the minister had to lean over the pulpit and whisper, "Bend his finger." Or on our wedding trip when the guard at the Canadian border asked to see my identification and I handed him my birth certificate as I nervously pointed out, "My name is Ann Sheetz but it's Kindig now because we're on our honeymoon." "Maybe you'd better practice that a little," he said dryly as he waved us on.

No pictures, either, of the ancient cars in which we took our dog for rides. No pictures of me caught in a manger with calves butting my back and our dog jumping in my lap. No pictures of us eating hot dogs on the Eiffel Tower and at German street fairs. No pictures of so many foolish but fun things.

And none, either, of us racing across Germany when a miscarriage threatened or of Loren's understanding when the doctor said, "No more trips until the baby comes or you will lose it." Or of the fun we had watching the Rhine because we couldn't go anywhere else.

There are pictures of Todd, and later Doug, when our prayers for a healthy baby were answered. But there are no pictures of the support Loren gave me as we watched our first-born wheeled out of an emergency room almost completely encased in plaster casts or as we watched doctors and nurses work to break the fever that wracked Doug's body in convulsions. "We'll make it," Loren said, and we both knew "we" meant "with God's help."

26

And there are no pictures of us buying a newspaper when we didn't know a Linotype from a press or of the joy we felt when "our" press groaned into motion as it began its first run on "our" paper, although I knew the idea had been mine. Or of my feelings as I felt responsible for our having quit two perfectly good jobs when our accounts payable soared ahead of accounts receivable. "We'll make it," became Loren's by-word and again I knew "we" included God.

Our marriage is in its twenty-fifth year. A quarter of a century. We're at the same anniversary Loren's parents observed on our wedding day. But there will be no gigantic double celebration because cancer and heart disease don't respect plans. And so, too, there are no pictures of shared grief in spite of our faith we will one day be reunited.

No pictures for a scrapbook. Only memories of laughter, tears, fights, reconciliations. Perhaps a blank sheet of paper is fitting. But with it will go a prayer in the name of him who blessed the marriage at Cana in Galilee. With his help our marriage will continue to endure the teasing and the fights, both ours and those of the two boys the practical jokers had in mind when they told us, "May all your troubles be little ones." And that we may continue to draw our strength from him who has buoyed us when days were bleak and the future uncertain except for his steadfastness.

CHAPTER THREE

Twice Blessed

Same Pattern

When our family of three became four, the doctor held up the screaming, red-faced, flat-nosed boy we named Doug, and I said, "Oh my gosh! I had the same baby again." He looked so much like Todd that time seemed to move back six years to the day another red-haired baby had been held up by a different doctor.

Baffled by this strange turn of events, we told our friends we were too poor to afford more than one pattern.

As the months went by, the resemblance became more pronounced: the same brown eyes, flat nose, big mouth, the same habit of crying in the early hours of the morning—surely no two babies could have been more alike.

The months turned into years; Doug's hair stayed red, Todd's became brown, then blond. Todd's hair gets long and clings to his head; Doug's turns up and forms little horns. Todd turns brown in the first sun; Doug stays fair all year.

Physical differences aside, we soon found other variations. Both ask a lot of questions but the timing is different. By the time Todd was five, he had asked where babies came from. Doug was four when he asked how they got out. Until he reached his teens, Todd thought girls should be forbid-

28

den at parties and any event considered "fun." Doug requested permission to have one boy and two girls help celebrate his sixth birthday.

Flying leaves Todd with stomach problems and hanging on for dear life; Doug smiles happily and sometimes sleeps through the trip. On the rare occasions we get them both in the family car at the same time, Doug feels too confined and becomes restless while Todd watches for big tractors and elaborate hog feeding operations.

Both are casual in their approach to clothing. Todd started kindergarten with four pairs of jeans and finished high school with four suits that he wears on those rare occasions he doesn't feel like wearing one of his two good pairs of jeans. Doug insisted on a sport coat, white shirt and tie for his kindergarten picture and for years was fussy about his clothes. He didn't keep them clean, but he liked to start out in good order. Now he considers himself the best dressed boy in seventh grade because he has four different styles of jeans.

At six, Doug still believed in the Easter Bunny and helped color eggs. Todd was twelve and protective enough to smile indulgently while he painted "Peace" on his eggs.

The only times they agree with each other are the times their father or I disagree with one of them. Then they become inseparable. But other than that, there's little resemblance to the original pattern.

It's been a long, hard nineteen years, and the next five probably won't be any easier because, while we thank God for the patterns he used, we pray for the help we'll need until Doug graduates from high school.

Of course, by that time Todd should be through college and married. Maybe we could just give him the pattern and let him worry about the results, learning for himself what his father and I mean when we pray, "Dear God, help us learn to live with our blessings."

If the Kid Grabs, I'll Bite

"Wow, Mom! Look at that cool car," my son said, pointing vaguely across four lanes of traffic.

"What car? Where?" I cried, bracing myself.

"Over there," he said disgustedly. "We just passed it."

My son had become a driver. After fifteen years of our taxiing him about, the state of Indiana determined he could drive if accompanied by a parent, and he took the driver's seat from us, relegating us to being passengers. This day was my turn in the ulcer seat, and I was too busy praying to have time to watch for "cool" cars. I watched for *all* cars—cars from the left, from the right, from behind, from ahead and, because I once saw a car fall off one highway onto another, I looked up a lot, even when there was no overhead road.

"Relax," he said. "There's nothing to it." His attitude was casual, his approach to driving businesslike. It was my attitude about being a passenger that was a bit uptight.

The first time I screamed, "Stop!" at the top of my lungs, he nearly stood the car on its radiator. Perspiration formed on his lips and brow. "What's the matter?" he gasped. I pointed to a car approaching from the right. It was a good mile away.

Neither of us said much after that. What was there to say? I rode in silence, only my eyes moving furtively from side to side, back and forth. Finally, I choked, "Take me to a doctor."

"Now what's wrong?"

"I just bit my tongue trying not to shout."

"Why don't you just sit there and ride?"

It sounded simple, and I tried, but how could I just sit there and ride? This was that cute little baby I used to let ride in the other bucket seat, the boy who later graduated

30

into a car seat complete with its own steering wheel. I thought it was fun to watch him "drive," I remembered as I recalled, too, how I used too grab him when I had to make a sudden stop.

That baby had grown so tall I could no longer look him in the eye but had to settle for his Adam's apple. He had the seat pushed back so far my toes barely touched the floor as my feet fanned the air for the brake that wasn't there.

You've come a long way, I reminded myself. This is just another part of his growing up.

Could be, but I figured the first time that kid grabbed me at a traffic light, I'd bite him.

Tooth Fairy Scale

"Look, Dad! I pulled a tooth," Doug said, poking a baby tooth under Loren's nose and pointing to his still bleeding gum.

"That's great," Loren said, backing away from the grimy hand that continued to wave the tooth. "You put it under your pillow and maybe the Tooth Fairy will leave you some money tonight."

"Aw, Dad, why don't you just pay me now and skip that Tooth Fairy stuff," Doug pleaded.

Somewhat taken back at this lack of confidence in the Tooth Fairy, Loren asked, "Just what is the going rate for teeth?"

"Twenty-five cents for little ones; fifty cents for big ones," Doug said, neatly pocketing the quarter and rushing to deposit money and tooth in his bank.

"High cost of living has hit everything," Loren grumbled as he returned to his paper.

His attitude must reflect that of other fathers. How else could one of our friends have become known as "The Cheap Fairy"?

It seems the couple had neglected to put any money

under their daughter's pillow. In the morning she cried because the Tooth Fairy had forgotten. Her mother quickly snatched a quarter from her purse, ran to the girl's room and, after a bit of fumbling, "found" the quarter under the pillow, quieting the girl's tears.

The girl was happy enough with the solution until she lost another tooth. Again her parents forgot about the Tooth Fairy. This time, however, her mother remembered it after the family had gone to bed. She rolled over and poked her husband. "It's your turn to be the Tooth Fairy," she said. He dutifully went upstairs and slid a dime under his daughter's pillow.

The next morning, after her father had gone to work, the little girl confided to her mother, "You know, I think Dad must have been the Tooth Fairy last night."

"Why?"

"Oh, you know."

"Know what?"

"You know he's kinda cheap about things like that," the eight-year-old replied. "He only left a dime. It should've been a quarter."

An eight-year-old Tooth Fairy minimum scale. The idea staggers the imagination.

Our Son Who Won't Be President

"Where do you suppose that thing is?" I muttered, aiming my flashlight at the bottom of a huge barrel I'd already emptied of baby clothes, dolls, wallpaper remnants, maps, high school papers, 4-H scrapbooks and a grotesque ceramic duck.

"If you can't find it, do I have to move out tonight?" Loren asked as I returned from the attic.

Ignoring him, I crept to the closet in the room in which Doug slept. I cautiously muffled the flashlight until I located a small chest behind the clothes, toys and card tables. There it was in the bottom drawer under an assortment of pictures and mending: our marriage license.

I carried it to the living room and dumped it on a pile that included Loren's and my birth certificates and a stack of legal documents.

At stake was Todd's citizenship status. Born in Germany where we lived while Loren was in the army, his birth certificate is in German, but he was admitted to the United States on my passport and later given a form indicating he was an American child born abroad. However, we were told that if he ever wanted his own passport he'd need a certificate of citizenship.

He wasn't planning a trip, but he was of draft age and while our own draft wasn't functioning and his conscription into the German army seemed unlikely, we felt it wise to get his certificate of citizenship.

Passport photos, a ten-dollar fee and endless forms later, we submitted copies of our own birth certificates, marriage license, etc. to the Bureau of Immigration and Naturalization.

Now the day had come. His hearing was set in federal court where, armed with the originals of the necessary documents, we appeared before a tired attorney. (Consider the thousands of youngsters born overseas and multiply them times an area extending from Chicago to New Albany and you can better understand his fatigue.)

We raised our right hands, swore to tell the truth and proceeded to answer questions, providing the proper documents as requested. (But after all my searching, we didn't need the marriage license.)

Todd signed a certificate of citizenship that will bear for all time his horrible passport picture and stood to swear an oath of allegiance to the United States. He promised to bear arms for his country if necessary and to defend it against external threat.

When he was through, the attorney said, "You have all the rights of a native-born citizen except one: you can never be president."

"That's okay with me," Todd replied as I reassembled the documents and stuffed them into my purse.

He's been a citizen since the day he was born, this son of ours whose ancestors first came to this country more than 300 years ago, but because of the location of his birth, the army can do to him and all the other thousands of children born overseas what the Republicans or Democrats can never do: draft him.

Adopted

As a first-born, I always took it for granted my parents had either found me under a cabbage leaf or purchased me from a stork. I never realized it was possible to join a family any other way. Adoption was not in my vocabulary. Therefore, I was totally unprepared when our youngest announced he wasn't ours.

It was lights-out time, and Doug had wound up his day by telling me of the dream he'd had the night before—one of having been adopted.

"How'd you like the idea?" I teased.

"It wasn't the first time, you know," he replied seriously.

"The first time for what?"

"The first time I'd been adopted. I know I'm adopted. You don't have to kid me."

"Whatever made you think that?" I asked. "I can prove you weren't."

"I think I can prove I was," he said, his face extraordinarily serious.

"How?"

"Just look at all the pictures you have of Todd. You don't

34

have that many of me. I wasn't around here when I was little so you couldn't take pictures."

"You were around," I assured him. "You and Todd looked so much alike at the same age that even your father and I don't know which of you is which in some of the pictures."

"Ha!" he snorted.

It is true that we have fewer pictures of him than of our first-born. Like most parents, we simply didn't take as many snapshots or keep up the baby book as well the second time around. If we had three or four children, I'm positive the last one would have to be content with his birth certificate and reprints of his siblings' pictures.

After a half hour spent trying to convince him he wasn't adopted, I found I was unable to alleviate his concern. He appeared troubled even as he slept.

"Where do kids get silly ideas like that?" I asked a friend later.

"I don't know," she said, "but I always figured I was adopted too."

And it's been the same every time I've mentioned it to a second-born. As children, they all thought they were adopted.

"How'd you react when you learned you weren't?" I asked one.

"I was horribly disappointed."

I never realized how much I missed by accepting that stork story.

But there seem to be compensations.

I found Doug and his father surrounded by a model kit, Loren clearly baffled by the hundreds of parts that lay in front of him. "If you weren't adopted, I wouldn't spend so much time with you," he teased.

Doug grinned broadly, feeling wanted even if he wasn't

completely convinced we found him under a cabbage leaf.
We never could get him to buy the stork routine.

Adaptability

"Mom, what's adaptability?" Doug asked.

I'd just adapted my tired body to the relaxing contours of the living room couch, and it was tempting to say, "Go away. Check with me in an hour."

Instead, I thought of our dog and found myself trying to define the word by illustration.

"You know how excited Herkimer gets when we go biking?"

He nodded.

"And you saw him when I went to the garage this afternoon. He ran in circles, barking."

He nodded again.

"But when the door opened, the rope caught your bike fender and the opener pulled it to the top of the garage."

He looked horrified as I continued. "And while I pulled your bike out of the rope, Herkimer chased birds behind the barn."

"Is that adaptability?"

"Right," I answered. "When he couldn't go right away, he switched to something else. And when he got hot on the ride, what did he do?"

"Rolled in a mud puddle."

"That was his way of adapting to the weather. He cooled off the only way he knew how."

"You mean adaptability is sometimes changing your plans a little to get what you want?"

"Sometimes it means changing them to what God wants, not what we want. And always it's changing them to new circumstances," I replied, plumping a sofa pillow and stretching my legs.

"That's interesting," he said, draping his legs over the arm

36

of a chair and sliding into a relaxed position as his brother came into the room.

"Hey, Todd, I know what 'adaptability' means."

"Yeah, what?"

"Well, you know how bad Herkimer smells after he rolls in mud puddles?"

Todd nodded.

"And you know how he and Mom both like to take naps after bike rides?"

Todd nodded again.

"Well, 'adaptability' is why Mom's taking her nap in the hot living room while Herk has the lounge outdoors in the shade. This way, they each get to rest. She's too warm, but she doesn't have to smell him."

"That's adaptability, all right," Todd agreed, eyeing the chair Doug was sitting in. "Why don't you be a good brother and bring me a glass of lemonade?"

"Only if you make popcorn tonight," Doug said, relinquishing his seat.

Todd grinned broadly as he took the chair.

"That was a dirty trick," I said.

"That was adaptability," he contradicted as he draped his legs over the arm and slid into a relaxed position.

Tree House Builder

Whatever it may be to anyone else, at our place evolution is a never-ending process that involves a tree house and a creative son.

The tree house was neat and functional when Loren built it. It had doors and windows, a floor and a roof. Lacking a tree of proper size, it was anchored to a huge elm stump where it provided a safe refuge for a six-year-old wishing to escape an infant brother who threatened his security as head man.

Time marched on. The tree house became a fort, a hide-

37

out, a barracks, a cage for a pet racoon. It was all things to two growing boys. But suddenly it was in peril. The stump rotted and the tree house tottered precariously. Drastic action was necessary.

"Tear it down," said Todd, then sixteen. With a driver's license, he was more mobile if Doug crowded too closely.

"Save it," said Doug. "I can use it."

We'd watched Doug grow into a sturdy ten-year-old whose strong hands had become capable of unlimited carpentry. We should have known he was really saying, "I'll work on it."

The once simple building was moved behind the barn where it grew and grew. Two wings and an upstairs were added. A ladder was built for cautious trips to the roof. Sliding windows boasted faded curtains. A discarded door from Grandpa's garage was cut in half and added, and gifts from many friends were worked into the design, so many, in fact, that Todd insisted everyone must hate us.

New inventions were constantly added to the tree house — it was always called that although it was never close to a tree. One was a pulley system to raise and lower building materials. A Doug Sheetz original, it involved rope, a pulley from the hay fork, ladders he built himself and a lot of ingenuity. But it worked. Like the tree house itself, it kept him busy for hours, his inventive mind constantly searching for new ideas and new ways to modernize.

The tree house was charming. I know that sounds like proud mother talk, because I know as well as anyone that no self-respecting hobo would have moved in — even Herkimer refused to enter — but it had a certain quality about it that made it precious. From the hundreds of bent nails to the ladder that topped the roof, it was Doug's. Every board, every bit of rope and string, even the rags that were supposed to cap holes in the roof, showed that a creative person, unencumbered by plans and rules and limited only

38

by his ability to make do with the materials at hand, had built the house. Hours of his development were represented — learning to use a hammer and saw, planning the effect he wanted, searching for new ways to improve it.

It was simple and very humble, but it was his and by being his, it was more than a loose pile of boards and windows. If a man's home is his castle, surely a boy's tree house must be his Taj Mahal.

Something I Ate

When they were two and eight, supper conversations with the boys usually ranged from, "Doug, get your feet off the table," to, "Todd, don't talk with your mouth full."

And when they were eight and fourteen, it was, "Doug, don't reach; we'll pass it, if you'll just wait a minute," and, "Todd, don't gulp your food."

"One of these times they'll carry on conversations," Loren would console me after they'd rushed off to more exciting pastimes, and I'd sigh. It seemed like an impossible dream.

But time changes many things. Doug is now a seventh grader whose sole course of study seems to be football, while Todd is a college freshman who likes calculus and economics, but more than anything is fascinated by sociology as taught by a Chinese professor.

Our weeks are hectic, what with meetings, printing schedules and football practice, and the three of us who remain seldom have time to say more than, "Hi." But on Friday, everything changes. The paper has been mailed, the bookkeeping is done, some of the job printing caught up, football practice dismissed early and our freshman comes home.

But Loren and I no longer talk much. The wonder is that we still try. But we do.

A typical Friday supper conversation now ranges from,

"Well, I got the posting done," to "I had a bit of trouble printing. The blanket kept rolling up."

"What kind of blanket?"

"Press blanket."

"Oh. Not like the ones they use for stretcher when someone gets hurt in football?"

"No."

"Did you know that in China it's considered a delicacy to eat the raw brains straight out of a monkey's head while he's still kicking?"

"Football's fun. Wind sprints aren't, though."

"I thought I'd never get the control to balance."

"I'd have gotten along better if I hadn't had to take time to put the wheels back on the turtle." (A large cart used in print shops.)

"He didn't say anything about turtles. He did say that monkey brains are supposed to make you smart."

"You'd be smarter if you didn't talk about that while we're eating."

"He said a lot of people like to dip mice in vinegar and then swallow them alive."

"Football doesn't take many lives, but it sure hurts a lot of kids. We've lost one in every game."

And there've been other changes, too. Not only are Loren and I talking less, I'm dreaming more. Like the other night when I had a nightmare about a marinated mouse being swallowed by a football player just before he was carried off the field on a blanket by a monkey whose brains were later eaten by a tired printer who rolled in on an out-of-control turtle.

It must have been something I ate.

Twice blessed. Two blessings. So alike and yet so different. In the name of him who said, "Suffer little children," we pray that we can. And they us.

40

CHAPTER FOUR

Generation Gap

Future Shock

Bite the bullet, quadraphonic, brown-bag, samizdat, stonewall, white-collar crime. Or, how about jet lag, mammography, ethnicity? A real potpourri of words, a mixed bag, some would say. What do they have in common? If the dictionary you're using is as old as the one I've lived with for fifteen years, what they have in common is that they aren't in it.

I'd been perfectly happy with my dictionary until Todd returned from his first week of college with a new paperback edition. I fingered its crisp pages, savoring the new words.

"That's a neat book," I said, and my family laughed. I leafed to the word 'neat' and found a slang definition: nice, pleasing.

Looking up words became fun, and I found interesting new ones, like schussboomer. Know what it means? A skier, especially one who schusses expertly. How about frag? To intentionally kill or wound a superior officer, as with a hand grenade.

"That's gross," Doug said when I read the meaning to him. I flipped to gross. "Very bad?" I asked.

"Yeah, it's very bad, but that's not what I meant by gross."

"What is gross?"

"Oh, you know, kinda super-yucky." I couldn't find yucky.

"That's sure a dorky dictionary."

I turned to dorky, but it wasn't there, either.

"How about bioclean?" I asked.

"Who cares?" he demanded. "The guy who wrote that must be a turkey."

"That's something to eat."

"Not always," he said, pausing as Todd came in, his eyes sparkling with excitement.

"You should have seen the humungus tractor I saw today. It was really tough."

I didn't know how to spell humungus (rhymes with fungus), but there wasn't anything even close. Tough meant something strong, that would not break if bent. I made the mistake of reading the definition.

"No way," the boys said as one. "Tough, like a tough girl."

"When I was in school, a tough girl was not a person either of you would want to know. Tough meant her reputation was bad."

"Far-out," they said, leaving me with the dictionary. I looked for klutz, which is what I felt like, but it wasn't there. I found small consolation that my own definitions and the dictionary's were similar for such words as bummer, ego trip and right on, but I couldn't shake the melancholy that accompanies the feeling of being detached from the world, watching it go by from the far side of the generation gap without really being a part of it.

"What's wrong?" Loren asked.

"I'll never be a schussboomer," I replied sadly. I didn't want him to know his wife was a person without a description.

"What's the matter? Can't schuss?"

I considered using the dictionary as a hand grenade, but

42

another word caught my eye. Future shock: an inability to cope with rapid social changes that have not been properly anticipated.

So that's what I'd been doing on the other side of the generation gap! It was of little comfort to realize that every lexicographer in the world was probably there with me, but it helped.

Toy Room

The generation gap at our house is filled with great bunches of knotted string, broken toys, collections of rubber balls, broken kites, bats and gloves, old magazines and catalogs, 500-piece puzzles with only 495 pieces, Tinkertoys orphaned from their sets, Erectorsets without nuts, games without instructions, science kits with only half the chemicals.

For years we called it the toy room; later, it became Doug's special domain. A room strictly off-limits for adults, it was originally intended that the doors could be closed when company came, but later they were flung wide open for all to see when the doors were needed to hold up other collections.

All generation gaps must be bridged sometime. We all face countless days of reckoning—the prodigal son had to chose to return before he could be forgiven, George Washington had to tell his father who cut down the cherry tree . . . and toy rooms, though less monumental than either, sometimes need to be cleaned, generation gap or not.

And it's usually a mother who does it.

Hard-hearted Mama. Sounding more like a drill sergeant than a loving mother, I yelled until everyone cleared the area and then attacked the accumulated debris with brooms and more determination than I really felt. Hours later, heaping baskets of broken toys, dirt, corn cobs and a pile of things I shuddered to think we had given shelter were ready for burning.

The boys were invited to participate in the carry-out detail. They were awe-struck when they looked at the sterile room that bore little resemblance to the place they had vacated only a few hours earlier.

"Do you see that toy box?" I demanded. "It's to keep toys in. Take good care of it. Keep it clean. Try to show some responsibility. I work too hard to have to clean up after you." My voice was becoming tinged with hysteria.

Doug, looking as concerned as only a five-year-old philosophical junk collector could, rubbed his chin and said, "That's probably true."

The remark was so incongruous, yet so completely appropriate, that I didn't know whether to laugh or cry, hug him or hit him, so I compromised by kissing both of them and apologizing. And they decided they'd accept my apology with some repentance on my part.

Luke says the prodigal son received a robe, a ring, shoes and dined on the fatted calf. The boys decided fit repentance would be a four-mile bike hike and, instead of rings and shoes, I ended the day with throbbing muscles and a deepseated conviction there must be better ways of bridging the generation gap than by cleaning and yelling.

Generation Gap

"I know what a generation gap is," Doug announced as he lounged in a lawn chair, carefully snipping the legs off an old pair of jeans for his first cut-offs of the season.

"You do?" I answered absently as I raked soil over newly planted flower seeds. "What is it?"

"Oh, you know," he said, "it's like Todd and I are the younger generation. You and Dad are the older generation. The difference is the generation gap."

"That's right," I said as I continued planting.

"There's one thing I don't know much about, though."

My breath froze as I looked at my eight-year-old. He knows the stork didn't bring him, I thought, but he doesn't know some of the really technical details. Here it comes. "What's that?" I asked, my voice barely audible.

"I don't know a thing about Shakespeare."

My sigh of relief was so great it blew away some of the flower seeds, but after I had regained my composure, I asked, "What did you want to know about him other than that he was a famous writer who lived many years ago?"

"Oh, what kind of stuff he wrote and about Romeo and Juliet and things like that."

"He wrote a lot of hard-to-understand things. I had to read some of his works in college, and I didn't like them."

"If I have to read Shakespeare in college, I'm going to quit."

"It's not that bad," I said hastily. "If you want to, you can read some of the things he wrote. We have several of his books in the house. Help yourself."

The subject was dropped, but after supper and a shower, he helped me select his first volume of Shakespeare and followed me around the house for help with words like Mr. Mustard-Seed and Mr. Pease-Bottom.

He became so engrossed in Shakespeare he took the book along when we went to visit friends, announcing immediately on our arrival, "I read Shakespeare."

He clutched Shakespeare in his hand all the way home, even after he fell asleep, and it was the first thing he looked for in the morning.

It would be wonderful to say ours was the only second-grader who read Shakespeare, but the generation gap wasn't as wide as he thought, and I saw him quietly slip the book back on the shelf. He didn't like it any better than I did.

There are many generation gaps. Some are filled with toys

and string, others with mutual regard for Shakespeare and still others with schussboomers and frustration. This isn't surprising since ours is a world continually divided into two kinds of people. Genesis tells us the story of Cain and Abel, the beginning of the battle of nomad versus farmer that continues in our generation. But there are others: black and white, liberal and conservative, haves and have nots, do gooders and care nots, parents and children.

And often this latter division becomes a dual role. My children's mother, I am at the same time my parents' daughter, and sometimes I'm certain "generation gap" means me. I love my parents and children dearly, but that very love is where the divisions often begin to strain, where feelings are hurt without intent.

But that love is the footing needed for the delicate bridge that spans the generation gap, one we pray we can provide, give and receive. And if ever we trod too heavily upon it, we pray for the courage of the prodigal and the love of the father to seek and to grant forgiveness.

CHAPTER FIVE

We Shook the Family Tree Too Hard

"**T**he difference between the right word and the almost right word is the difference between lightning and the lightning bug."

That quotation from Mark Twain is pinned to my bulletin board, and I stare at it often as I deposit lightning bugs in my work instead of the words I seek. But it's a good saying and I keep it there even as I continue gathering lightning bugs.

And besides, I'm supposed to be related to Mark Twain. No one knows for sure, but they think he and my great-grandfather were second cousins. Hardly my next of kin, but tantalizing enough to make me want to know more about my family, although an old Chinese saying better expresses it: "To forget one's ancestors is to be a brook without a source, a tree without a root."

I didn't want to forget. I wanted to know who we were, where we came from.

But when I became an amateur genealogist, planning to trace Loren's and my family trees to their very roots, well-meaning and more experienced friends cautioned, "Be prepared to find anything. Every family has something unusual in its background. Don't be horrified at anything you find."

Armed with that bit of disquieting information, I proceeded in my usual enthusiastic style to research both trees at the same time. The result was confusing, but interesting.

Especially when one surname, Swartzlander, continued to reappear in each of our families. His was Philip; mine was George. Born a few years apart, they lived in the same area, and their children came to Indiana at the same time.

As months wore on and the two Swartzlanders appeared to grow farther apart, so did the two Sheetz boys. After a few fights, I threatened to take my half of the Swartzlanders and leave if they didn't quit arguing. And Loren threatened to take his half after a couple more sibling-type brawls. Both boys decided being brothers was a drag; they liked their cousins better.

In spite of the fighting, I put aside my relationship to Mark Twain and concentrated on the Swartzlanders. Diligence and research paid off on a visit to the state library when I found records indicating one Johannes Phillip Swartzlander had come to the United States from Germany in 1752. He had many children, including a son Conrad. It took more research and several exchanges of letters before we learned Conrad was the father of both Philip and George.

Now we had something. For one thing, we had Todd, born in the same part of Germany his great-great-great-great-great-great-grandfather had left more than two hundred years before. But even more interesting, we had a lot of cousins. For instance, I had Loren; he had me, sixth cousins. Neither of us can take our half of the family and leave; we'd still be stuck with the other half. My brother's children and his brother's children are cousins. My father-in-law was my cousin and my father is Loren's cousin. Loren's nephews are my cousins and so is my brother-in-law, and Loren can claim as cousins my brother and his children.

But what really appealed to the boys was the knowledge that they were cousins, albeit seventh cousins, and the fighting actually slowed for a few days while they reflected on being more than just brothers. They became so confused that Doug, then nine, decided he was his cousins' uncle.

Who knows? Maybe he is. I threatened not to go another twig further with my research. But curiosity, coupled by a man able to take me back seven more generations on one line, got the better of me, and I learned some of my ancestors came to the United States more than 350 years ago. I also found out that I might be related to Queen Elizabeth of England and to one of the astronauts. But I haven't gone much further, stopped by the realization of the truth of friends' caution that we could find anything if we shook the family tree too hard. I found a sixth cousin to whom I'm married; it's hard to tell what his cousin might be.

It's sad, really. No longer can we glare at each other when one of the boys misbehaves and say, "He got that nasty temper (stubbornness, etc.) from your side of the family." Or, as the boys finally summed it up when the novelty wore off, "Gee, since it's all the same family now, it's a real drag."

But when I feel too put upon by the cousins who are also my husband and sons, I look again at my bulletin board and see another quotation from that cousin not yet researched, Mr. Clemens-Twain: "Martyrdom covers a multitude of sins." True martyrdom doesn't, of course, but what about the kind I exhibit when I demand of those cousins, "How can you do this to me, after all I've done for you?" "I slave over a hot typewriter all day and what thanks do I get?" "Isn't anyone going to notice that I waxed the furniture?" "Why can't we eat out at least once a week since I work so hard the rest of the time?"

Jesus did not say the way would be easy. Neither did he say being a cousin would be easy.

CHAPTER SIX

Give Us Our Daily Peanut Butter

Peanut Butter and Carrots

It is 4:45 P.M. of a typical working day. My desk is a mess; my mind is racing to figure a way to get it all done by five when the telephone rings. My son's excited voice shouts, "Mom!"

I grip the edge of my desk. One of them has cut his leg off and the other has run away from home. No, someone's calling; the other one must be dead. "What?" I shout.

"We're out of peanut butter! Get some on your way home."

Weak with relief, I hang up the telephone, scoop up the rest of the work to do later and go in search of peanut butter. Not just any spread will do. It has to be a specific brand and it must be chunky. None of that smooth, creamy stuff for these boys.

My sons are connoisseurs of peanut butter. In this day of specialization, everyone has his thing. The boys' thing is peanut butter.

They don't eat it on their cereal or their cake or anything like that, but they do have their little specialties, inherited, no doubt, from a father who absolutely loves peanut butter and tomato sandwiches. They aren't big on peanut butter and tomatoes, but have you ever heard of peanut butter and brown sugar?

I'll never forget the first time I saw one of those sandwiches. It looked like sand-covered garbage. "What is that thing?" I gasped.

"Peanut butter and brown sugar," Doug said, peeling off the top slice of bread. "See."

I saw. The peanut butter was half an inch thick and was topped by an inch of brown sugar. My stomach reeled.

Todd is more sophisticated, he tells us. He prefers peanut butter on celery with lots of salt. You can imagine his disgust recently when he learned we were out of celery. "What'll I do?" he asked. "All we've got is a lot of carrots."

"How do you know you don't like peanut butter on carrots until you've tried it?" Loren asked facetiously, and before you could say "Jif," the boy had smeared peanut butter on six carrots and munched them down.

"How are they?" I asked, and he mumbled, "Kinda crunchy."

"Peanut butter coated bananas are supposed to be a delicacy," I said. "You might try one if you want something quieter."

"Right on," he said, dousing a banana with a heavy coating of his favorite spread.

"How's that?"

"Carrots are better," he mumbled, licking peanut butter and bananas from the roof of his mouth.

Before you could say "crunchy," both boys and their father were eating carrots smeared with peanut butter. I maintained I was the only sensible person in the foursome and watched in silence.

Actually, I had just remembered melting peanut butter over popcorn when I was much younger. I thought it was pretty great then, but now it seemed better to be quiet. I didn't want to end up demonstrating—or eating peanut butter on a carrot.

51

The Kids Who Are Eating Us Out of House and Home

"The chicken we had for dinner was delicious," Loren says, reaching into the refrigerator for a midnight snack but finding only an empty plate. "Where'd it go?" he asks.

"Your number one son took it with him to eat on the way to the ball game."

"He get the macaroni and cheese, too?"

"No, Number Two got it before he went to his friend's house."

He shakes his head and settles for a carrot and a piece of celery. At our place, you have to be fast if you want something to eat.

There was a special on potato chips and I bought six cans. Supper was late and in desperation I remembered the chips, but it was too late. Only a crumb showed they once were there. Leftover ham that would make sandwiches for four dwindles to a soup bone overnight. Tuna salad disappears as if by magic, leaving only a trail of chopped eggs and a touch of mayonnaise to show it existed. Half a chocolate cake in the morning means an empty plate by night. A carton of ice cream can be traced on its route from refrigerator to wastebasket by dibs and dabs smudged on the cupboard.

"Who ate the cheese I needed for supper?" I ask, and the oldest replies, "Motor Mouth took it with him to the woods."

"Who got the last bottle of pop?" Loren asks, and the youngest replies, "The kid who never carries out the trash drank it before he went to his meeting."

Empty bread wrappers, well-scraped peanut butter jars and drained milk cartons greet me on my arrival home from work, a scant hour after the bus has deposited the walking appetites I call sons.

It does no good to ask who emptied the cartons, because

there is never anyone to ask. The kids who are eating us out of house and home are never home.

Blueberry Blurp

Every family has its culinary specialty—beautifully roasted prime rib, extraordinary barbecued spareribs, or outlandish baked Alaska. The list could sound like an epicurean delight.

But, I suppose, every family also has its "thing," the dish that somehow never turns out quite right.

My mother has always been a beautiful cook, and I can think of few things she's ever made that have been less than perfect. But, put her recipe in the hands of another cook and anything is possible. If you doubt this, you should have seen the cakes my brother used to make with her recipe. Even the dog found them inedible and more than once we found a lumpy and pitiful imitation of Mom's version lying at the bottom of a bin of wheat where our loyal pet had buried it.

And after Loren and I were married, I had plenty of failures with her recipes, learning the hard way that her cherry pie recipe called for canned, not frozen fruit, and suffering with yeast dough that either raised too much or too little, coffee cakes without baking powder that were like life without laughter—very flat. But it wasn't until recently that I perfected "my thing."

It was a cold winter Sunday and one of the boys brought a friend home after church. We were all in a hurry to go away and dinner was all but done when I discovered there was no dessert. I had a lot of frozen blueberries so I dumped some into a baking dish and sprinkled on the same topping I use on apple crisp, hoping the dessert would bake while we ate. Repeated trips to the oven showed little progress so I continued advancing the temperature control, not stopping until the 500 degree mark was passed. By the time I put the dessert, still in its glass baking dish, in the center of the table, it could only be described as volcanically active.

It was too hot to pass so I served the dessert while everyone added his own ice cream, which melted immediately, forming little streams of milk in the bubbling mixture. Bubbling? Blurping was a better description. What remained in the dish bubbled up and popped with a blurp, sending everyone into gales of laughter until the next blurp.

Of all the desserts I've made that turned out right, that even vaguely resembled the picture on the recipe, what do they still want? Blueberry blurp. It's the specialty of the house.

Garage Sale Gourmet

I went to a garage sale recently and bought a $20 cookbook for fifty cents. It is a gorgeous, huge book with over a thousand pages of recipes. It's still so new every page crackles and the dust cover's picture of a copper kettle of white sauce and a pile of dewy fresh vegetables has not faded.

The newness should have told me something, but I failed to get the message, only wondering why none of its pages stuck together like the ones in my other cookbooks. It's easy to tell which recipes are favorites in our old, familiar cookbooks because those pages have splatters of dough and batter and smudges of chocolate that tend to glue themselves to each other. Not so with this new cookbook. It's so clean it's frightening.

I brought it home and over a cup of tea fingered its clean pages, savoring the definitions of terms I had never understood, like *coq au vin* and *truffle*.

Suddenly I sat up straight and realized I had just read instructions for cooking a cock's comb (*crête de coq*). You pierce a fresh comb with a needle, squeeze it between your fingers as you run cold water over it to remove the blood

54

and then "cover it with cold water and put pan on lively heat" and leave it there until the water reaches 104 to 113 degrees. At this temperature, the skin of the combs begins to detach and can be removed. This is no simple process, and the cook is advised to rub the combs one by one in a cloth sprinkled with fine salt until the skin comes off. After being soaked again until white, the combs are plunged into a boiling white court-bouillon and cooked thirty-five minutes. They can be served as hors d'oeuvres or used as garnishes if skewered. Makes bacon-wrapped chicken livers and parsley sound pretty old hat, doesn't it?

Further reading has provided recipes for blood pudding, cow's udder, and all forms of camel—feet, fillet, hump, paunch, ribs and pilaf.

But the camel is not a native of Pucky Huddle. I turned to the section for rabbit, expecting something more exotic than hasenpfeffer, even as I knew none of us could actually bring ourselves to shoot one of our cottontails. No matter. Rabbit in this book is identified as hare and defined as a wild rodent. Somehow, this takes it out of the game class and puts it in the rat and mouse category. But even rat is described as edible, especially those nourished in wine stores and grilled over a fire of broken barrels. At least the book has the decency not to give the recipe.

Nor are recipes given for giraffe, hippopotamus or dog, although each is described as being considered edible by some people. There are lots of recipes for eel, including one with a picture that looks like a coiled snake.

Feeling a little squeamish, I poured another cup of tea and went in search of peanut butter. But the boys have been asking, "How long until we have something out of that new cookbook?"

They'll get something. I don't know when, nor do I know whether it will be *croquettes d'amourettes* or *Quenelles de brochet mousseline,* but one thing is certain — the pages of that book will never stick together on cock's comb or eel or blood pudding or camel hump.

Romans says nothing is unclean of itself, but if a person thinks a thing to be unclean, it is. Which is why I choose to give thanks with my sons for their daily peanut butter, not condemning those who partake of rats or eels but thanking God we do have a choice — even if it is sometimes peanut butter and carrots or blueberry blurp.

CHAPTER SEVEN

In Sickness and Health

Pre-Formed

Being basically a healthy family, it's seldom one of us is in the hospital. Still, I have become acquainted with emergency room procedures, have known the sensation of realizing the ambulance's red light and siren are for one of us and the sickening realization that traction equipment can be used only after a hole is drilled through a small boy's shin. My small boy. And I've tried to hold my husband's arm quiet, the one with the intravenous tubes, while he hissed through parched lips, "If you really want to do something, get me a glass of water."

But worst of all is waiting for one of them to come out of the operating room.

It was a sunny Friday in July, and Doug was in surgery. Eleven, going on thirty, he was the bright-eyed optimist, the constant worrier. The intense one. The one who knew all the answers. "Cousins shouldn't get married," he once announced seriously. "They could have pre-formed kids."

I tried to relax. It was only tonsils. But well-meaning alarmists had told me about children who died during tonsilectomies or later developed heart murmurs, and I worried. When they checked our family background, the information was depressing. Heart trouble? Both sides. Cancer? Dad's side. Diabetes? Both sides. Kidney problems. My side.

And then I remembered my genealogical research and the disquieting knowledge that Loren and I are sixth cousins. No problems genetically, but did this compound all those "yes" answers on the doctor's chart? Did we, as Doug would say, have a "pre-formed" child, one with two families' medical histories squeezed into one boy? By then I knew if he survived, he would have leukemia, need daily insulin the rest of his life and it would be only a matter of time until his first open-heart surgery or kidney transplant.

"Why does it take so long to remove one set of tonsils?" I asked the coffee machine, wishing it could answer.

But, finally, the nurses wheeled my son back to his room, and I rushed from the waiting room to be with him.

"Tests all okay?" I asked, a tremor in my voice belying my calm.

"Just great."

Doug's lips moved and I strained to hear. "I wish I'd never had it done," he gasped, and I wanted to laugh and cry at the same time. Instead, I clutched his hand tightly.

He glared at my hand on his and his lips contorted in an effort to speak. "If you really want to do something, get me a glass of water."

And then I knew—he was pre-formed after all. Like father, like son. A chip off the old block.

"Oh God, thank you for my pre-formed son," I whispered as I noted the birds still sang and the day was still bright. "Thank you, thank you," my heart screamed as I went in search of a nurse.

Domino Theory

I never really learned to like dominoes. It seemed too laborious to try to match dots; I preferred standing them on end, side by side, and, lightly touching the first, watching in fascination as they toppled.

58

At ten, I didn't realize this was the "Domino Theory," a term favored by government spokesmen because it has a more pleasant connotation than to say that if one country falls, another will follow suit, just like a string of dominoes.

But if the theory works on governments like it worked on our family when Doug came home with the flu, the thought is positively frightening.

He complained of nausea when he returned from a party. "It was great," he exclaimed, "except the last hot dog tasted sort of funny."

"After a dozen, it probably did," we laughed, bundling him off to bed in hopes sleep would quiet his queasy stomach.

It didn't.

We found him wrapped in a blanket on a couch in the living room, his face white as the sheets he'd spread under him.

And on Monday night we found his father in the same position, a dishpan at hand in case of emergency.

By Wednesday night and for most of Thursday, it was my turn in our family's favorite but least private room in which to be sick, the living room. I ached and chilled as I jogged to the bathroom.

And by Friday, the spot was occupied by Todd, his head buried under pillows so no one could see how he looked. He subsisted on chicken noodle soup and television.

It was a long, hard week that left no one in the mood for games. Except the one who set the family into motion, domino style. "What'll we do this week?" he asked at breakfast Monday.

"We'll keep an eye on you," we said in unison.

"That doesn't sound like much fun," he grumbled. "Why don't we plan to play games some evening."

"Such as?"

"Well, I never learned to play dominoes right. All I know how to do is stand them on end and watch them fall over when I push one of them."

"You know enough. Now's the time to learn to make them stand up again."

"Why?"

"Generations of people have toppled them. No one has ever gotten them to get back up on their own."

"Sounds like a silly game, if you ask me."

We're going to have to explain to that boy that God gave us hands for many reasons, not the least of which is helping up those felled by the domino theory.

Seven-Letter Word

Measles is a seven-letter word that is supposed to affect its victim three days. In reality, the victim and his family feel its effects almost forever.

By the time we knew we were going to have measles for New Year's (we'd previously had mumps for Thanksgiving, chicken pox for Christmas and appendicitis for Father's Day), we had managed to expose more relatives than we cared to count.

Even worse, Todd broke out at his grandparents' house where he stayed while we combined two days' work into one to put out an early paper.

Working mothers tend to think they have failed when a child comes home from Grandma's looking like he's been sprayed with red paint. Grandma doesn't mind, but Mom does. It's one of those times she'd gladly trade her typewriter for a steady job on the family hearth. But by then the kid's already speckled and there's nothing to do except nurse him back to health.

Without doubt, the surest way to forget all your resolutions about tolerance and patience is to spend four days with two boys, one of whom feels miserable and crabby while the other feels like a million dollars.

Doug made a fishing pole out of an Erector set and dangled it at Todd. He tickled him, swiped his pillows, laughed at his spots and lorded it over him when he got to accompany his father to take pictures of a train derailment. In the meantime, Todd was made more miserable by missing trips to friends' houses and being deprived of television and reading. I spent my time reading aloud and playing games with Doug, the healthy yet neglected one who refused to play with his Christmas toys." "I want to keep them new," he said.

In spite of our care to make him feel wanted, Doug felt so rejected we heard him say, "I hope I get the measles. No one likes me anyway."

It was a happy day when the spots finally faded. The New Year started looking brighter and I never looked forward to returning to work so eagerly in my life.

But there was coughing from the other half of the gang, and we began preparations for measles on Valentine's Day.

How to Enjoy Being Bedfast

Peace, the loudest, most boisterous peace in the world, reigned at Pucky Huddle when Todd returned from spending five weeks in traction in a hospital fifty miles from home. We rejoiced that part of his long ordeal was over and we tried to put out of our minds the horror we'd felt when we learned he'd been struck by a car. Or our self condemnation for our two-worlds idea that enabled him to go to the library after school instead of coming home. Or our concern that people would say we'd never taught him to look both directions before crossing a street. Incongruous as it seems, that's the thought that kept crossing my mind while the state policemen questioned us about the incident.

Doug, then only a little over a year old, had spent the five weeks peering out the window where he had seen Todd board the school bus. He'd shout, "Todd!" at the top of his lungs and when his brother failed to appear he'd climb in a chair and glare at a picture of the two and yell "Todd!" a bit louder as if to say, "Get out of there so we can play." He pointed to his brother's empty bed and yelled again, and he looked for him in odd places. But when he saw him come home in an ambulance and wheeled into the house on a stretcher, he took one look at the heavy cast and reacted by backing away and staring in horror at his disappointed brother.

By the next morning, Doug had managed to scale the end of the borrowed hospital bed to look Todd over a little better. By noon, he climbed in bed with him and Todd, with tears of joy in his eyes, hugged and kissed him soundly.

By evening, home was back to normal, plus some. Doug had discovered Todd's new "bedside bathroom equipment" made good nesting places for dominoes and crayons. He discovered he could take the register out of the floor and throw marbles, puzzles, pencils—anything Todd might want—down the opening. And, best of all, Todd could yell at him but he couldn't chase him. He also found himself sitting on a chair a good bit of the time.

And while our cup was running over with joy, we were little prepared for the three months it would take Todd to go back to school and the demands his convalescence would place on our imaginations. It was then I learned the A-plus I had earned in college for a set of activities to entertain a sick child was almost completely worthless.

The cards failed to take into consideration that seven-year-olds are not unduly concerned about broken legs, nor are they fascinated by sedentary activity.

If I were to take the course again, I would subtract some

of the more inactive games and substitute some Todd devised. Such as:

1. *Go Fishing.* This is fun and can be done with a bent clothes hanger for a fishing pole, a big supply of rubber bands, a bit of ribbon from a gift package, a hook off a broken toy and anything you want for a fish, although wooden building blocks work fine. There is only one problem with this game. The block won't stay on the string, no matter how many times you wrap rubber bands around it. But this is okay. It gives your mother or babysitter something to do and you get free entertainment while they crawl under your bed to retrieve your "fish."

2. *Rebound Mama.* This could also be called Rebound Daddy or Alice or Grandma or Grandpa. All you do is fill in the name of the person staying with you. You need sharp reflexes for this game. You wait until she gives you a drink of water and straightens your bed. See her off with your most engaging smile and get ready for the really hard part. And it is hard, because you have to time it perfectly. You wait until you hear her get to the top of the stairs or go in the bathroom or answer the telephone or go outdoors. Then you yell for her at the top of your lungs. This will bring her every time, and she'll get you a book or crank up your bed or tune the TV—if she doesn't get mad and crank you down, turn off the TV and make you take a nap. With practice, you can develop a knack for hearing the smallest squeak of her chair at the supper table, the click of her typewriter, the rustle of her newspaper, her bed as she climbs into it or the door as she opens it. The main idea of this game is to never, never let her get everything you want on the first trip. The more trips the better. It makes you feel secure and it makes her feel needed.

3. *Mailbox Ears.* This lets you hear the crunch of the mailman's car on the drive as his car nears the box and you

can begin clamoring for someone with two good legs to get the mail.

4. *Become an Elf.* This goes along with No. 3. You join this fun club on TV with the sick elf leader and you refuse to watch any other channel, because, as your club card warns, you'll get your eyes poked out if you watch the others. You can watch for the mailman for days until he brings your badge and credentials. It's fun to wear the badge on your pajamas, but if you admit that it pokes you, you could lose it.

5. *Love Her a Little.* After you've tried all the other ideas and she looks as if she could fall on her face, call her to you and say, "I love you, Mama," and give her a little kiss on the cheek. Ten times out of ten, she'll kiss you and squeeze you and tell you you're one of the two most wonderful boys in the world and that she is so lucky to have you. But if you're not careful, she'll gook it up by crying. If you don't like too much hugging and kissing with a little crying, you'd better be ready to swing your fishing pole because it's time to start all over again.

But Todd finally graduated from his cast to crutches and soon he was walking again, even attempting to run. For some reason, he joined Little League that summer, limping heavily as he ran the bases. He'd never before been interested in sports, nor has he been since, but the exercise was good for him. We rejoiced at his determination, giving thanks in the name of him whose legs were not broken that our son had been returned to us, for the doctors who had healed and for the joy we all shared when the hospital bed was returned and the "bedside equipment" sold at a garage sale.

CHAPTER EIGHT

Time Is a Dirty Word

Law and the Soaps

I'm in trouble most of the time. The deadline for "Odds and Ends" is Friday, but often it's not written until Tuesday or Wednesday. Some weeks, nothing seems funny and I settle on reading instead of writing.

Actually, I never intended "Odds and Ends" to be humorous. I meant it to be serious, like the book I'm reading, the one that makes me cluck impatiently and wonder if I can ever learn to write like that, knowing full well that covering the meetings the writer describes would be boring beyond belief.

But I do go to meetings, and not long ago I found myself at one in which one woman stood out. She was clearly the most beautiful person in a room populated by American and foreign journalists. Sleek and sophisticated, her bearing clearly bespoke a sharp mind honed by years of education. My assessment was verified when she was introduced as a lawyer-turned-journalist who covered Parliament, wrote in-depth studies of the Bahamian educational system and had a regular column. I felt like Charlie Brown in the presence of the Great Pumpkin. But I was brought up short when the woman making the introductions confided, "And Jeanne writes the only television serial indigenous to the Bahamas."

A soap opera written by a lawyer! I'm as easily bored by soaps as by some meetings, but I gave this tall creature my undivided attention and heard her explain that actually her column was "only a fortnightly thing" because it would be difficult to do it more often. A person after my own heart!

Later, at the home of a mutual friend, we found ourselves seated together as we balanced plates of spaghetti. I was at loss for words, but finally I asked, "Is your column serious?"

"Oh no. That would never do. It's light and funny."

"Why did you choose humor?"

"Parliament and some of the meetings I attend are such bores . . ."

"And the soap opera?"

"It's funny, too."

"Why?"

"Because that's the only way you can get a message to Bahamians. If you give them something serious, they'll sit there and suck on their teeth."

So that's what I was doing when I clucked over the book! I tried a new line of questioning. "Are you basing your column in the States while you're here?"

"So far I haven't had time. In fact, I was up until three this morning and my back's killing me."

"You had to work that late?" I asked. Even I seldom stay up until three.

"Not really. I had to finish Agatha Christie's new book."

A soul sister!

I persisted with my questions. "I suppose you wrote the serial ahead?"

"I'm only two weeks ahead right now, and I'll have to work all weekend. I can't decide whether to take the central family to America or leave them there. One actress wants out, so I'll have to kill her or have her move."

"Sounds like a lot of work. Does it pay better than law?"

"Only about a quarter as much, but it's much more fun."

"Are we Americans different than you expected?"

"I understand you better now than I did before I came. Your problems are more evident. But what about you? Do you understand the Bahamian way of life?"

"A lot better than I did yesterday," I replied.

I hated to tell her I couldn't see that it was any different from ours.

A Day Like That

I'm the person writers have in mind when they write advice on how to get a lot of work done with little effort. I thrive on such tidbits as, "If you really want to get a lot accomplished in a short period of time, you will begin at least three jobs at the same time. You can take down the bedroom curtains, clean the bathroom and polish the floors on the same day if you will start all three jobs at the same time. You will hate to go to bed without the bedroom curtains and will get that job completed just as you will finish the floor because who wants to go back on the same place two days in a row. Ditto for the bathroom. The object is to get a lot of things going at the same time."

Marveling that someone else would write advice that sounded so uniquely mine, I set aside a Saturday to salvage our home from encroaching filth.

I started upstairs by stripping all the beds. And since washing bedding is mainly letting the machines do the work, my agile mind quickly moved to other things that could be done. It would be a good time to clean floors, I decided, but when I went in search of cleaners I found the window spray which reminded me I'd better clean the living room windows.

But the first window was not only dirty, it was new, having replaced one recently broken by an energetic son.

Its putty had not been painted and the frame looked tacky. It was a nice day; the upstairs could be cleaned at night or on a rainy day but there would never be a better day for painting than the present. I went to the basement for paint. If it hadn't been such a nice day, I never would have made it back, what with the toys, empty fruit jars and discarded boots that give meaning to the water softener man's day on his bimonthly visits and threaten our limbs daily.

By the time the paint was stirred, it was time for lunch and I almost lost my enthusiasm, but the smelly substance brought the truth of the article into focus. I couldn't ignore it, so I painted—the windows and doors and myself, the porch floor and the boys who refer to me as Mom. I had so much fun painting I forgot everything else, even the poison ivy that grows in the wild honeysuckle, although I had occasion to remember it a few days later. In fact, it seemed for a while that the memory would be more durable than the paint, but it didn't matter. I had set into motion a chain of work that would keep me busy the rest of the summer, because now the trim on the rest of the windows looked tacky.

But the day I had started was not yet over. I ached in every joint, giving myself over to the mercy of a hot shower and planning to go to bed early and outline a novel. One look at the upstairs told me the novel would have to wait and convinced me of the truth of the article's advice. You do have to finish something. Not a bed had sheets or blankets. The washer and dryer had long since stopped, but I had failed to notice.

Still, you couldn't say my Saturday was a loss. I had done the article one better, ending with four things to show for my time instead of three. We had clean sheets because I did have to re-make the beds, we had a window and two doors that looked a lot better, I had poison ivy and a set of aching muscles.

A day like that can't be considered a total loss.

Cleanest Grapes

Most housewives will tell you that the best way to get the house cleaned is to plan guests. Nowhere does that hold true more than in our house.

Saturday was not only the day of the planned guests but also the day of reckoning for a house that had accumulated papers dropped chairside, books left open where the reader left them and assorted old-fashioned dust and grime. As soon as we shooed Loren out, the boys and I set to work. Todd burned trash, tied paper, vacuumed, dusted, even straightened his room. Doug pushed everything into one pile in his room and covered it with his bedspread. I washed the plastic grapes.

Actually, I wouldn't have noticed the grapes were dirty if it hadn't been for a paint sample I found in an accumulation of circulars. One color looked like it would be nice for the family room we don't have, but I wanted to see how a collection of colored glass would look with it. It was while checking the glass that I noticed all the dishes in the hutch were dirty. After I had washed them, the inside of the hutch and all the things sitting in the window, marveling at how we could collect so much stuff, I found there was still enough water to wash something else. I threw in a handful of plastic grapes that had sprouted whiskers. They rinsed beautifully. Real ones never looked better. I dried them by shaking them and plopped them back in a hanging planter. Water ran down the wall. Rushing them to the kitchen, I put them on the drainboard. Two hours later water still ran from them and I moved them to the utility room where I could

69

watch them while doing the laundry.

While Todd continued cleaning, I discovered the grapes were completely filled with water and, feeling more than slightly idiotic, I carefully squeezed each until it was drained.

Minutes before the guests arrived, I plopped the grapes back in the holder and held my breath. Only a slight trickle appeared.

Amid greetings on a porch that should have been swept and trying to wedge coats into a closet that hadn't been straightened, I knew without doubt that although the kitchen floor was still dirty and the dining room windows were filthy, we had the cleanest plastic grapes in the county.

I don't think anyone else noticed.

State Fair

Every family has a different approach to attending the state fair. Ours is not one of togetherness. Years ago, we determined we were happier if Loren and the boys spent the day on the machinery field while I studied quilts and art, resting my feet at style shows. They could marvel at new combines and farrowing arrangements while I examined the photography exhibit. It works beautifully — when we let it.

Notice of a meeting I wanted to attend at the Indianapolis Zoo came as we were making plans for our yearly trek to the fair. "This year, I'm going to be sensible about the fair," I announced. "No more litter and debris. No more aimless wandering. I'm going to leave you guys at the fair and go to the zoo. That way, when I get back, I can see my favorite exhibits in two hours and we'll be ready to come home. It'll be much less complicated."

The meeting at the zoo was interesting, the speakers stimulating. The luncheon was good, even when I discov-

70

ered a pair of gigantic boa constrictors watching every bite I ate.

But in spite of my avowed intentions, I found myself clock-watching. A tour of the zoo was announced; I declined. "Have to meet my family at the fair." A camera safari led by one of the state's top photographers was likewise refused; my camera was at home, and besides I didn't have time.

With an hour to spare before time to meet my family, I parked the car and took off at a semi-trot for the manufacturer's building where I inched around the displays, marveling at how slowly lines move, failing to really see anything. Finally putting that building behind, I loped off to meet the clan. I was already exhausted from the near trot, but they were rested. Loren had escaped the burning sun by sitting in a display corn crib while the boys examined tractors and stone pickers. They were delighted by what they'd seen; he was relaxed. It was a good combination.

They granted me my second hour, which I spent rushing back across the infield to the horticulture building and then back to the 4-H exhibits. I met them precisely at the specified time, and we left.

In the two hours I'd allowed myself, I'd crossed the fairgrounds three times and had been in four buildings an average of fifteen minutes each. I hadn't seen the quilts, the art, a single style show and not only had I missed the photography exhibit, I'd missed a camera session with a really good photographer. I hadn't seen the zoo, and I hadn't seen the fair. Instead of killing two birds with one stone or, in this case, taking in two events with one trip, I'd missed them both.

And then I knew why it takes a day to see the fair and why it makes sense to sit through style shows or in corn cribs. Proverbs 19:2 tells us, "He that hasteth with his feet sinneth." Translated into 20th-century vernacular, that could mean "some things just can't be rushed."

Countdown

"Only two years, one month and a day left until I can get my driver's license," Todd remarked when he blew out fourteen candles on his birthday cake.

"Yeah, and it's two months until my birthday," our then almost eight-year-old said, "and boy is it going to cost you guys a lot this year. My birthday is on Easter. Two kinds of presents."

"Just wait until you get older," their father admonished. "You won't look forward to birthdays so much. You'll look forward to other things."

"Like what?" they asked.

"Like a lot of things," I said absently, letting my words and thoughts trail off because they weren't really listening anyway.

NASA didn't originate the countdown; Adam and Eve did. All of life is just a big countdown. Before we're born, our parents count the days until we will be. After we graduate from diapers and nursery school to ruled yellow pads and pencils, we count the days until we graduate, get a job, get married, have our first child. After he's here, we count the days, weeks and months until he gets his shots, adds new foods, goes to school. Multiply it by the number of children you have and the countdown time is endless, kind of gruesome, really. We count the days from birth until death. . . . I tried not to think about it.

"I can't wait to get out of school," a boy was saying. "Me either," the other echoed. "Only a week until the tourney," one of them said.

Loren looked at his watch and said, "Only an hour until bedtime," and they scrambled off to watch television.

"Kind of quiet, aren't you?" Loren asked as the sound and fury left the kitchen.

"Just wondering how long until I can do all the things I've always wanted to do," I answered. It sounded inadequate.

"I know," he sighed. "I'd like to fly more, farm more, print more. Not enough time."

"Hurry here, hurry there," I groaned. "No time to read or write."

"We should have been twins."

"Right."

"Maybe in two years, one month and one day we can get a chauffeur."

"Gee."

Borrowed Time

I never really understood the ominous sound of the words, "He's living on borrowed time," until a storm put out our lights for a quiet hour after supper one hot summer evening.

When the storm was over, we resumed our lives as normal and a few days later someone remembered to re-set the kitchen clock, but no one got around to the clock in the living room.

It would have been a great week if I hadn't awakened so achingly tired every morning. "I'm not getting enough rest," I told my family. They nodded. They'd heard the same refrain many times before.

But the nights were deliciously long and offered such great possibilities. For instance, there was always plenty of time to take short drives after supper with time to spare for reading. I should have realized the situation the night we got home at eight and I settled in for reading, heaping praise on the boys when they returned some time later by saying, "I'm glad you made it by eight."

It's not that I didn't know the clock was off. I did. But it was so easy to forget. And so complicated. I'd go to bed and discover it was midnight when I had intended to be asleep by eleven or I'd awaken in the morning convinced it was actually the alarm that was off and roll over for another hour.

Late to bed, late everywhere. It would have been a miserable week if I hadn't been able to accomplish so much. But the day finally came that I re-set the clock, barely able to see the hands for lack of sleep.

Borrowed time? Keep it. I can't afford the interest.

Deliver me, Lord, from myself, from my self-imposed subservience to a four-lettered word that too often rules my life — *time* — and help me come to know that it is only when I quit taking each day as it comes and start committing each day to you that I may view time for what it is — a glorious opportunity — instead of an obscenity.

CHAPTER NINE

Stress Opens the Door

Pillow Maker

"**W**hatcha doing, Mom?" Doug asked suspiciously as I snipped zippers from the covers of our toss pillows.

"Saving money," I answered as I pricked my finger with a pin in an attempt to loosen a thread.

"We still going to have pillows?" he asked sadly as he watched the worn covers land in the wastebasket. They represented a lot of his development. He could remember being sick on the turquoise one, using the brown one to slug his brother, and the comfort of crying on the avocado one. Both boys had long ago learned the orange one was softest and the tan one the hardest, and they had fought like tribal warriors over possession of each.

"We'll have pillows," I said, directing his attention to a pile of bright fabrics, remnants of years of sewing.

"Cool," he said. "I want the pretty ones."

"They'll all be pretty," I answered. "Homemade is in."

Feeling highly creative, I wondered vaguely if I should be writing, but I decided to take a Saturday off and brighten my home.

Slowly, the material was turned into new covers, and as they were carried to the living room I could hear a chorus of complaints. "You've got the prettiest one." "So what? Yours is bigger." "What happened to the orange one?" "I think it's gold now, but I'm not sure."

I broke two sewing machine needles, emptied countless bobbins and snapped thread and patience equally. Still, it was with a great sense of accomplishment that I viewed eight new pillows.

"Not a bad day's work," I sighed as I sat back to admire my handiwork. The results pleased the boys, and they settled on the couches, heads cradled by bright, new pillows.

Taking my cue from them, I tilted back in my recliner and picked up a magazine. Flipping through the pages, I found an article about the tornado that only months before had devastated much of our area. "That's a story I should have done!" I yelled as I recalled the hundreds of pictures I'd taken, the peanut butter cookies I'd made for the workers and the miles I'd walked watching and helping with the dramatic clean-up. And who could forget the way no one cried, only did what had to be done? Or the truck that hadn't run for a year but carried a man to safety after he started it on the first try? Or the Amish and Mennonites who came to help total strangers and the feeling that, even in the midst of desolation that rivaled battle scenes, God was with us, helping?

"Maybe the author didn't have to make pillows," Todd said, breaking into my memories of the wind that in seconds had ripped apart centuries of man's attempts to harness the soil with homes, factories and towns.

I smiled at his simplistic view, realizing ruefully that my attempts to maintain our best of two worlds lifestyle often resembled the tornado's path as it plowed across the country. Here a little, there a little — not the same path of destruction, but surely the same random hit-and-miss way of touching down.

I sighed again and closed the magazine. So our way of life

does have a few warts, I thought. It's a way of life worth preserving, one in which priorities must be met. Today we'd needed pillows. There would be other articles and, in the meantime, I had supper to prepare and another load of clothes to wash.

My ever-present work was no longer as threatening as it had been a few years earlier when I had found myself nearly incapacitated by indecision, frustration, anger, resentment and jealousy. At least now I could be philosophical, but there had been a time I would have been reduced to tears by the pillows, by the work undone while I made them, by the article someone else had written. And they hadn't been tears of joy but tears of bitterness and frustration that threatened my marriage, my family and my very life.

Symptoms of Trouble

As one of those rare individuals who early accomplish all their life's goals, I should have been shouting with joy. Instead, I fought back tears as I huddled miserably in the doctor's examining room, folding and refolding a slip of paper.

"What's this?" he asked as I shoved the paper at him without waiting for his usual greeting.

"A list of my symptoms," I gulped.

"That's quite a few," he said.

I nodded miserably as he read the 12-point list that began with lump in breast and ended with tired all the time. I was grateful he neither laughed nor dismissed my complaints lightly. A breast examination revealed that in spite of the fact two of my friends had recently died of cancer I was not likely to be the third. A shot would clear a troublesome infection, and if I'd come months earlier I could have avoided the leg aches that had left me limp with pain. One after another, I heard him return "nothing wrong here" verdicts to the items on my list.

I blinked back tears and waited for other tests, expecting him at any minute to declare me a hopeless hypochondriac easily influenced by my friends' illnesses. Instead, I found myself on his treatment table having an osteopathic adjustment. Bracing myself for his next move, I prayed he wouldn't break my neck. Instead, for the first time in months I could move easily and with little pain.

"Not bad," I said as he finished, the first words I'd managed without tears.

"How long has it been since you and Loren had a vacation?" he demanded.

"Not since we bought the paper," I replied, hating the tears that washed my cheeks and dripped onto his pillow.

"How long since just the two of you went out for dinner?"

"I don't know," I answered, trying not to sob.

"How long since you just sat back and let the world go on by?"

"I don't believe in that. The only way to get ahead is by working. I have a family, a home and a paper to care for."

"If you don't get yourself pulled together, you aren't going to be around to enjoy your family or your home or anything else," he said. "If you don't learn to relax, you could be dead in a month."

"Is that all you can tell me?" I asked, pointing to the list. Being dead in a month had not ranked high on it. I may have feared cancer, but I had no intention of dying right away. "Sorry, I don't have time," I joked, my smile giving way to tears as I realized what I'd said.

I cried all the way home and for the next three days, shutting off the flow only long enough to visit with people who came to the office on business, hating myself that I could present a happy face to them and nothing but tears to the men in my life. Finally, I told a woman what the doctor had said. She looked at me sympathetically and asked, "Did he say what you'd die of?"

"I didn't ask," I wailed.

I cried and prayed, pleading with God not to let me die. "I've got too much to do," I told him. "Just give me strength to conquer this."

Tears finally gave way to determination. I would not die. I wouldn't die just to show the doctor who was in charge.

"Surprised to see me?" I asked a month later as I eased my aching body onto his treatment table.

"Should I be?"

"You told me I could die in a month," I said. "I didn't." My smile did little to camouflage the tears that threatened.

"You might not die for years," he said, "but you could feel like you had. You could keep going at this frenzy until you simply could not function for a couple of years."

"A couple of years?" I gasped, and he nodded. Death was almost preferable to a two-year limbo. Imagine the work that would pile up. I shuddered involuntarily as he began kneading my painful back and neck.

"Ever lose your temper?" he asked.

"Not for a long time. I used to blow up at the least little thing. Lost a lot of friends that way."

"What do you do when you get angry?"

"Try not to show it."

"Do you know you're really only bottling it up?" he asked. "It's all right here," he said, poking an especially sore place in my neck. "You've got to get it out of there. You've got to release it."

"It would only hurt someone."

"Not as much as it's hurting you."

It was several months before I could stem the tears long enough to ask, "What are we working against or on or whatever?"

"Stress."

"You can cure it by poking and snapping me?"

"I can't cure it. That's up to you. I can make it less painful. You'll have to find a way to avoid creating the pain."

"And if I can't and your adjustments don't help, what then?"

"Medication."

"Tranquilizers?"

"Probably."

"No thanks, I'll pass."

"If you had diabetes, you wouldn't hesitate to take insulin, would you?" he asked, still flexing my back, still demanding I relax.

"That's different. This is something I want to work out."

"Just remember, some things can't be worked out alone. You'll have to do most of it, but you'll have to have help."

"What you're telling me is that I can cover demonstrations, interview senators and nurse my family's ills but I can't cope with my everyday existence?"

"You're building too many mountains out of molehills. They're tripping you up."

"Do I need a psychiatrist?"

"The biggest part of psychiatry is listening. I'm willing to listen."

We both knew I'd climbed one of those mountains by asking the question without tears, and I was relieved by his answer. Past experience had taught me he did not refuse to recommend specialized treatment when cases warranted it. Evidently mine did not.

But I was not ready to talk, and besides, I was trying new ways of relaxing — even if the results sometimes left something to be desired . . . .

Some People Never Relax

Stress, I had found, was a six-lettered word for an affliction that bothers most of us, one whose sole treatment is an elusive ten-lettered word called relaxation.

Sixteen letters. Between them, they account for a multi-million dollar business that sells 16,000 things guaranteed to help us relax, but that really specializes in advice, often caring only for the symptoms, not the cause.

Relieve stress by meditation, says one article, while another admonishes that meditation is sacreligious, self-destroying. Still another, like my doctor, advises losing your temper. "Fight. If someone irritates you, tell him or her so." And the next article, written by someone of my persuasion, says, "He who loses his temper loses much, including the respect of his fellow man. It is a sign of weakness."

From other articles I found lists of suggestions I pinned to my bulletin board:

1. Plan some idleness every day.
2. Listen to others without interruption.
3. Read books that demand concentration.
4. Learn to savor food.
5. Have a place for retreat at home.
6. Avoid irritating, overly competitive people.
7. Plan leisurely, less structured vacations.
8. Concentrate on enriching yourself.
9. Live by the calendar, not the stop watch.
10. Concentrate on one task at a time.

Or:

1. If the worst happens, it happens. There is a difference between worry and concern, but don't worry.
2. Forget the past.
3. Live well today.
4. Learn to be content with what you have.
5. Put your primary trust in God and not in yourself.
6. Pray regularly.

"The trouble with you is you read too much," Loren said as he watched me stare at the bulletin board, one hand already moving to another pile of books.

My eyes ached so badly I agreed a change of pace was needed, and we surveyed the possibilities with little success. I'm a poor gardener. My musical ability is a minus nil. I never could master the use of knitting needles.

"Have you ever done anything besides read?" he asked finally.

"Well, I embroidered dish towels when I was ten," I said after some thought.

"Try embroidery."

"I wouldn't embroider another dish towel if my life depended on it."

"Isn't there something else you could embroider?" he asked so plaintively I said I'd try.

That's how I happened to take up crewel.

My helpful husband stapled fabric tightly over stretcher bars and sat back to watch as I picked up my needle. And speed. Especially speed. Every muscle in my body concentrated on the new stitches, and I determined that by working steadily I could finish the picture in less than a week and be free to read. I sat up until 1 A.M. two nights in a row as I worked so fast the chrome burned off the needle.

Loren said, "I thought this was to help you relax," but he bought me a new kit and more needles, ducking every time I swung the long stretcher bars of the massive project.

My new hobby was declared unsafe to life, limb and light bill.

"Maybe if you just sat under a tree and did nothing," Loren suggested.

"Maybe," I said, thinking of a new book.

"Like now," he said, guiding me to a chair that was soon shrouded by a swarm of mosquitoes bent on tapping my tense body for blood.

"I'll fog the yard," he said.

82

But quicker than you could say, "Skat!" our junior mechanic raced to the mower with the fogger attachment. "Needs oil," he said.

One poured oil, the other fogger solution. I swatted.

"Woops! Spark plug's shot," Doug announced.

I swatted and waited.

A lusty roar indicated repairs were successful, and soon the entire yard was blanketed by dense fog. I couldn't see a thing as I raced to the house and slammed windows shut, too late to keep out the clouds of insecticide that billowed in the evening air.

"You can come back out now," they called fifteen minutes later. I opened the windows and returned to the chair.

The evening was quiet. I leaned back, closed my eyes and concentrated on not concentrating. "Ah, this is relaxing," I purred as another mosquito bore into my leg.

"Must not have gotten all of them," Loren said, heading back to the garage.

"Forget it," I yelled as I ran to the house and grabbed a book on how to escape stress.

"What got into her?" Doug asked.

"Some people never learn to relax. She's one of them."

No Laughing Matter

But it wasn't a laughing matter. I couldn't relax. There was always so much to do. And seldom was anything done the way I thought it should be. "We are not running a taut ship," I screamed at Loren, finally losing my temper, releasing months of pent-up hostility that did not all have to do with him.

"Rome wasn't built in a day," he said calmly.

"Neither was Pucky Huddle," I shrieked. "But Rome and Pucky Huddle both declined, fell away from their former glory."

"You've been to Rome. You know that life continues there, that new buildings are constantly being built. You live in Pucky Huddle. It may not be the settlement it once was, but it has four worthwhile people living in it, and new buildings occasionally go up here, too," he said, pointing to the garage that had replaced a delapidated hen house.

He was right, of course. But why was I never right, never able to cope? Never able to explain my misery?

I felt reduced to nothingness, an absolute blob of nothing. What I didn't realize was that the door to my spiritual closet was about to open. And, luckily, I had no way of knowing how painful that opening would be or how absolutely nothing I would become before the door swung.

Instead, I concentrated on what would happen if one of my closet doors really opened and a visitor could see the mess that lurked within — the clutter that piled up in spite of sporadic attempts to create order.

"I'm a failure," I told myself as I tried to keep up with my self-imposed schedule. My mother had managed to get up at 4:30 every morning to help with the milking. By 5 P.M., she could be found back in the barn, sometimes by herself if Dad was busy with field work. In the hours between, she made most of the clothes either of us wore, even shirts for my brother. She raised huge gardens that she canned for our winter meals. And she kept a spotless house.

Surely I, who seldom had to get up early to help with chores unless we happened to have calves or lambs not yet weaned, could manage. But I couldn't. I loved to plant seeds, to work in the soil, but I hated to hoe. Even worse, the produce was always ready for jars or freezer on press day. So there was no garden. No cows, no garden. My sewing was limited to occasional slacks, even rarer dresses and blazers. No cows, no garden, little sewing. True, these were offset by editing a paper, attending meetings, club participation and nightly battles with homework, but Mom had had her share of the latter, too. So why was my house never clean? The obvious answer was that I was seldom home. Why? Because there were always too many things to do, too many meetings to attend, too many affairs the editor really should see about.

Even worse, the same answer was used for the people who asked why I was seldom in church. "But don't worry about me; I'm doing fine," I assured them. "I pray constantly. I have a good relationship with God."

I didn't tell them my relationship was confined to a closet of Detroit's making, the driver's seat of my six-cylinder car. The engine raced frantically every morning, rendering the vehicle undriveable for a few minutes after it was started. Ever conscious of time, even reduced to dusting the telephone as I talked, to crawling under the desk for more dust if the conversation did not require note taking, I found myself praying while I waited for the engine to warm up. And like Abraham of old and the scribes and Pharisees who demanded one from Jesus, I watched for signs. If, by the time I finished praying, the car ran smoothly, I decided God intended me to have a good day. If it didn't, I figured I either hadn't prayed hard enough or had used lightning bugs instead of the right words. Spotting a cardinal was considered positive proof God had heard my plea and had sent my favorite bird as a sign.

Expecting receipt of my prayers like a return on a registered letter was ridiculous, but it buoyed me through rough days of overcrowded schedules, fatigue, envy of those who took vacations, jealousy of any woman who could make my husband laugh, something I seldom seemed able to do during those bleak months.

"God is faithful," I read in Corinthians. "He will not let you be tempted beyond your strength, but with the temptation will also provide the way of escape, that you may endure it." I drew comfort from the words, but I was troubled because I had also read Christ's admonition: "I am the way, the truth and life: no man comes to the Father but by me."

But I was trying to, because, while I professed to be a Christian, albeit a closet model, I found it difficult to accept a lot of what I read about the man called Jesus. I resisted the idea that Jesus had withered a fig tree for not bearing fruit. It sounded like a temper tantrum to me, and I worried what would happen if he decided to wither me because I didn't produce when he thought I should.

Most of all, I was repelled at the notion that Christ died for our sins. "If he did," I said, "it was a waste of a perfectly good life. We're all so sin-filled that he accomplished nothing."

"Accept what you can on faith, the rest on reason," a minister told me, and I promised to try. If the Son of God had power in my life, if there was anything more than fable to this story, it would have to enter on reason and reason alone. Faith was an intangible. I reacted only to tangibles, things I could see and feel or even sense.

And so I continued to try to reason with God, asking him to show me visions, give me signs he heard. Nothing. "I want to accept Jesus along with God," I told a friend, "but I want to see him, to feel his presence."

"It sounds more like you're waiting for the Second Coming instead of wanting him to enter your life," she said dryly. "Don't forget that Hebrews tells us faith is the substance of things hoped for, the evidence of things not seen."

Reduced even lower in spirits by the truth of her statement, I felt the muscles in my neck tighten. God had not created the stress; I'd done it myself with my insecurities, my anxieties, my drive to excel. But, in spite of my doubts, I knew there was only one doctor who could heal it, who could provide the help my earthly doctor said I needed.

I turned again to my church after being absent many years. Sturdy structure that it is, the walls didn't collapse. The people were friendly, and I entered into the spirit of the services, which soon centered on a lay witness program. The team members' stories were moving and I wept as I listened. I longed to share their belief, but reason held me in my seat when it was time to go forward. "People will laugh," I worried. "My parents will wonder where they failed. After all, our whole family joined church together; we all accepted Christ together. People will question why I need to accept him again." And so I remained in my seat, crying. And I wept all the way home and for the rest of the afternoon. "They that sow in tears shall reap in joy," the Psalmist tells us, but all I knew was there was something I wanted badly but I couldn't let go and reach out. It was there, but I had to make the move.

"Services like that play on your emotions," someone said later, and I replied, "But it was so close, like something I could feel."

"Maybe you want to see or feel too much."

"Maybe."

Even more impatient with myself, I stayed away from church again, wrestling with the conflicts that raged within, rationalizing that I got as much comfort from going to the woods on Sunday morning and telling my problems to the trees or from riding my bicycle to the lake as I did in going to church.

The Door Swings

Talking to the trees and riding my bicycle may not have helped me eventually return to church, but the physical exertion required to pedal up the hills erased some of the stress, and I found myself looking again at the lists on my bulletin board.

Plan some idleness every day. A big order, but how

wonderful it was when I finally could sit quietly in the porch swing and watch cloud formations. How rewarding to lean back in my recliner and rest my eyes, knowing full well I'd fall asleep but cherishing the nap.

Listen to others without interruption. I never interrupt, I thought, but I found I did. Impatient with people who took too long to tell a story or who groped for words, I filled in the details, leaving them sitting quietly while I talked. Treatment would be painful and would continue for life.

Have a place for retreat at home. My spiritual closet in the car was eventually replaced by our den and still later by a little office Loren remodeled for me at home, a one-woman place where I can write—and pray. "Mom's pad," the boys call it. I've come to know it as a place of worship, of rededication, an oasis in which I can work or pray without interruption by telephone, teakettle or dryer. It's a luxury, really, because the car worked fine, but there was always the nagging thought, "I should be going to work." A place alone creates few pressures, only time for solitude, however brief, in which to communicate with God.

Plan leisurely vacations. One of the most important goals, it's one still unfulfilled, because our staff is too small to double for us if we both leave at once. Instead, we've had to settle for occasional weekends off, short family outings that require little time or money. Stress is not alleviated by having to work night and day for a month to catch up from a week off, and our vacations are still in the future. But we give thanks for Pucky Huddle, our own refuge, even if the work is always here and the horseweeds and thistles grow faster than our suntans on the rare days we sit in the lounges. And, sometimes, not setting the alarm is a vacation, a respite.

Live by the calendar, not the stop watch. This was the hardest rule to follow, but the most rewarding after I tried.

88

It meant re-evaluating every activity in which I was involved—not overlooking washing dishes or pasting up the paper. I found the reason for my stress often lay within me—that I was creating problems by scheduling two interviews in the same afternoon, by planning to attend a meeting one hundred miles away and an early dinner for the same day, by inviting guests for the day after I'd met a deadline for a special section and then staying up all night to clean.

I looked at my calendar and found penciled in many meetings that added little to the item entitled enriching yourself—or that practiced the Golden Rule. I've always been bored by meetings, stifled by committees and frustrated by discussions that are tabled month in and month out. But I pursued many of them because I felt it was my civic responsibility to be active in the community.

The realization that I was doing the clubs even less good than they were me hurt, but it made writing letters of resignation easier. I could truthfully say I would miss my association with the members but my schedule would not permit me to continue as a member. My calendar didn't clear overnight, because there are always many meetings to cover for the paper, which, because of school consolidation, covers a much larger area than it did fifteen years ago. But not a single subscriber complained that I no longer served on two refreshment committees in the same afternoon, rushing from one meeting to another with one eye on my watch and the other in the rear view mirror. Eventually these bits and dabs of time accumulated until I could arrange an afternoon a week to either watch clouds, clean, nap or bake surprises for my family. Not a bad bonus for being a quitter.

Concentrate on one task at a time. Always a dedicated list maker, I found I could not discontinue living with memos, but I could stop making them while I ironed or pasted up the paper or prepared for guests. And, even more importantly, I found that washing plastic grapes counts for nothing, almost as little as praising myself for painting windows when I really need to wax the floor. Or that sometimes it is better to leave all these things undone and simply go biking with one or both of my sons.

The suggestion that was most helpful was *if the worst happens, it happens.* That means if my mother sees dirt on my windows, she sees it. It's not the end of the world; she'll still love me. If Loren runs away with another woman, he runs away. I may not like what happens, but if it happens, it happens. Going on is what counts.

Forget the past. Isaiah told us not to call to mind the former things or ponder things of the past, but it's hard to put away old grievances, harder still to forgive our own trespasses. It was only when I understood what is implied in the Lord's prayer when it says, "Forgive us our trespasses *as* we forgive those who trespass against us," that I realized how little forgiveness would be coming my way. I had forgiven few of the people who had hurt me, however real or imagined that hurt may have been. And I'd forgiven myself none of the sins I'd asked God to forgive. Following the rules to prevent stress would not be easy, nor are they yet, but I'm trying, and trying is better than holding grudges. And it hurts a lot less.

Live well today. Committing each day to God is the only way to live, but God gave us free will, and that is where we run into problems. And it explains why God hears such plaintive prayers from me as, "Help me handle this interview." "Don't let me eat another piece of fudge." "Help me resist that bowl of corn chips." They're javelin prayers — short and to the point — but they help me cope, to meet each day as it comes, even as I commit it to one who never

90

heard of corn chips but showered manna from heaven. And he showers me with guidance I'm sometimes too tired to see, that's there, day by day. But it took me a long time to learn I could depend on it, to know *I* was the *him* Isaiah meant when he said, "Thou wilt keep him in perfect peace, whose mind is stayed on thee."

Learn to be content with what you have. Actually, although I had accomplished my life's goals, the realization was frightening. I don't mean a "Gee, what else is there to live for?" attitude but a "Gee, is this it?" knowledge that I had achieved my basic goals without ever having clearly defined them. I had never said where my house would sit, what kind of books would line its shelves or what kind of personalities my husband and children would have.

Therefore, I shouldn't have been surprised to find my home doesn't overlook a river, its yard is covered with dandelions instead of edelweiss, and rabbits, not gazelles, range the rocky fields around it. Or that our books tend as much to flying and crafts as to Proust, or that my husband prefers printing, flying and farming to art galleries, first nights—or newspapering. Or that my sons prefer farming to everything and think gourmet cooking is chicken every Sunday and hamburgers and French fries all the days between.

And I hadn't actually thought about the kind of person I woul be. At twenty, we don't often think how we will look at thirty or thirty-five or forty. Oh, we may see "that woman" in our mind's eye, but we don't even describe her in our diaries because it's something sort of super-personal. Then one day we look in the mirror and we don't like the graying, dumpy reflection that scowls back. At least I didn't, and I set out with tints and diets to perfect that reflection, but it did not improve. Instead, I found a hungry redhead with patches of hair that looked more pink than auburn peering back from above a miniskirt. I hated her more than I disliked the dumpy brunette with streaks of white. It was a case of not winning for losing—in more than one sense of the word.

I resurveyed my assets and found our best of two worlds idea was working, even if the boys had rejected half of it, even though Loren had come to like the job printing portion of our business better than the newspaper, even if I felt myself to blame for his unhappiness in a world of newsprint, interviews and deadlines. These are my worlds, and I like them better than I like their worlds, but it doesn't keep all our worlds from merging on a common meeting ground—our home. This is where our love for each other is still expressed, more often in actions than in words, and where we can all restore from the frustrations we feel in each of our worlds.

In fact, when I begin to thank God for my blessings, I often say, "I hope you aren't too busy, because I've got a lot to be thankful for." The list seems endless, but the day I found it was about fifty times as long as my petitions, I wept with joy and humility. Humility is a funny word, one a slogan warns, "If you think you have it, you've lost it." But it is also the state of being humble, and humble was how I felt when I resurveyed my assets. Humble and contrite.

It's hard not to be materialistic in our society, just as it's hard for me not to envy friends and family who fly to the Orient, Africa or Europe. Some day, I remind myself. In the meantime, there is so much to be thankful for that nit picking about not getting past Pucky Huddle's rock-strewn fields seems a bit unreasonable.

Put your primary trust in God and not in yourself. I couldn't do it. I was used to handling my own problems, thank you. I couldn't remember a time I hadn't prayed for strength to handle difficult situations, for courage to tackle

92

assignments, but putting my primary trust in God was something I could not do.

My doctor's advice haunted me. "Some things can't be done alone. Sometimes you need help.... Psychiatrists listen.... Talk...."

I was at the end of my rope. There was nothing physically wrong with me but I was miserable in spite of my best efforts to help myself, in spite of having at least partially succeeded in checking off a list of man-made suggestions for eliminating stress.

Instead of going to a psychiatrist, to my doctor or even turning to God in another of my "now hear this" prayers, I called a friend and invited her for tea.

The value of calling a Christian friend for tea can't be overemphasized. It not only provides a welcome break in both your schedules but a chance to witness or admit the weakness of your faith without fear of not living up to someone else's expectations or embarrassment because of your tears. My friend and I are kindred spirits who draw sustance from Romans 12:15: "Rejoice with those who rejoice, weep with those who weep." We dare not look at each other in church after a beautiful anthem or a powerful sermon for fear we'll dissolve in tears.

And we not only weep with each other, we listen to each other. On this particular day, she did most of the listening, because I had reached the point I could talk. And I did. All my doubts and frustrations were aired, even the silly, petty ones.

She neither laughed nor retreated into a spiritual closet. By the time she left, I had learned the meaning of Jesus' words, "Where two or three are gathered in my name, there am I in the midst of them." He was with us in the den when she told me I had to put my primary trust in God. "You can't do it alone," she said, sounding vaguely like my doctor. "You

93

have to have help. God is that help. God will never let you down. God won't change prescriptions. God doesn't require drugs. God can take over your whole life. All you have to do is let him."

"Just like that?"

"Just like that. He doesn't demand you have all your theological beliefs sorted out or that you have read and understood every word of the Bible."

"How will I know he has heard?"

"You'll know. That will come later. What you have to do is make a definite commitment. You have to tell him you can't handle your life. He knows you can't but you have to admit it."

It was a big order for someone schooled since infancy to believe anyone could do anything if he worked hard enough, and it wasn't until I was again in that closet of Detroit's making that I could bring myself to follow her advice. I don't remember what I said, only that I haltingly confessed to God that I could not handle my life, that it had become too complex even with the simplifications I'd made. "Take it to use however you can," I prayed.

I don't remember if the engine ran properly after that or if I saw a cardinal, but I do know I felt a gigantic burden had been lifted. From all I had read about people who turned their lives over to God, I had come to believe I would feel nothing right away. Instead, I felt at peace for the first time in years, even as I realized that in yielding fully to God, I had accepted Christ—and his death. The enormity of the love God has for us is overwhelming. I felt, as I always will, very unworthy of such love. And I realized, too, that Christ had withered me as surely as he had withered the fig tree. He had forced my old self to die that I might enter into his life for myself and come to know the resurrection as God's yes to man's no.

Galatians had new meaning when I read: "I have been put

94

to death with Christ on his cross, so that it is no longer I who live, but it is Christ who lives in me. This life that I live now, I live by faith in the son of God, who loved me and gave his life for me."

And I wonder if Paul wasn't thinking of stress victims when he wrote, "Be anxious in nothing, but in everything by prayer and supplication with thanksgiving, let your requests be known unto God, and the peace of God which passes all understanding shall keep your hearts and minds through Jesus Christ."

This is the place I should say that fully receiving Christ in my life ended my battle with stress, and it did, although I still wrestle with schedules and my doctor says I'm about as relaxed as a telephone pole. "But you're better," he adds, and I only smile and say, "Of course. You didn't think I was going to keep paying you all my hard-earned money, did you?" It's hard to come right out of the closet and tell your doctor you called in a specialist because you felt the need for a superior physician.

But it's not hard to see that the door is opening. I'm back in church—because I want to be there, because I know now a church is a hospital for sinners, not a showplace for saints. And I'm participating, sustained by the Psalmist who wrote, "He that goes forth weeping, bearing the seed for sowing, shall come home with shouts of joy..." (Psalm 126:6 RSV).

I was burdened and heavy laden. I sought rest and received it. Having received it, how selfish of me it would be not to take Paul's advice to Timothy, "Be not ashamed of the testimony of our Lord."

Or as my friend said the other night when she saw me dab my eyes as I told another friend that turning to Christ is the only answer, "It looks like the door is opening on our closet Christian."

I pray it stays open.

CHAPTER TEN

The Family That Hobbies Together

I t's cheaper than nerve medicine," the craftswoman said when I arrived for an interview.

"Better for you, too," I replied as I prepared to photograph her hobby—designing and making exquisitely decorated eggs, richer by far than Fabergé's famed jewels. Just looking at the delicate creations made my nerves snap to attention, but not so my new friend.

"Once I start working with eggs all my problems disappear," she said.

I know the feeling. It's one that comes from being a dedicated hobbyist, whether it be a macramé artist working out frustrations in knots or a pilot who leaves his cares on the ground for an evening of flying around the pattern or over the reservoir.

Some women get the same release from scrubbing their kitchen floors on their hands and knees. The rest of us hobby.

And some of us make it a family affair. . . .

You Go First, Mom

"You go first," they said, those brave sons of mine who had joined their father in convincing me that soaring was what I really wanted to do.

I climbed into the glider with the grace of a cow climbing

a fence, muttering that what I really wanted to do was take my Sunday afternoon nap.

Helping hands fastened straps around me that resembled a parachute harness. "I'm not going to jump," I said.

"Just making certain," they teased.

With my feet stuck straight out in front and the harness securely locked, there was little left to move except my hands. I waved them bravely at my family as the tow plane accelerated and our glider whished down the runway.

"We're now going about forty miles per hour," the pilot said as the glider lifted off the ground even before the tow plane had taken off. It was a strange feeling to be higher than the craft towing us.

It wasn't long, however, until the airplane was off the ground, towing the glider higher and higher. Like water skiers, we followed the plane's pattern. By the time the altimeter said 2300 feet, the pilot decided it was time to cut loose from the tow plane. "Pull that red knob in the middle," he said from the rear seat. I'd never been a passenger in any craft that let me sit in front, and I wasn't sure I liked it, but I obeyed his command. A loud bang told us we were on our own.

I'm not sure what I expected. Something like the awed reaction Loren's nephews had the first time he took them flying. One boy looked around as the plane climbed through a cloud bank and asked in surprise, "Where's Jesus? We're in heaven but I don't see him."

I didn't see him either, but I could see the world God had created, and it was beautiful. The only sounds were my heart beating three-quarter time and the light swish of air.

"See that shadow over there?" the pilot asked. I nodded. Shadows mean clouds and clouds mean rough flying for light planes below. A cloud may look like a puff of cotton but the air around it can kick.

"We'll get under the cloud," he said. "I think there should be a thermal there."

I didn't—and still don't—understand thermals completely, but I did know thermal did not refer to a warm blanket but to a mass of air rising from the ground. Glider pilots like spring because of the thermals that rise from plowed fields. Fields that have recently been mowed or combined are second best. Least favorites are corn fields because the thermal activity is not as great over foliage.

"Ah, yes! There it is!" he said. "Do you feel it?" he asked, manuevering the glider in tight circles, now rising, now dropping slightly, now circling, then back up.

"Yes," I replied. I hated to admit what I felt was my stomach tickling my wisdom teeth. I don't circle well.

We climbed another 400 feet, circling tightly to keep within the confines of our thermal. It was the highest flight of the afternoon, he said. Between circles, I learned his name was Carl and he had once soared from Lafayette, Indiana, to St. Louis, Missouri, a seven hour flight. This time we were only at 2700 feet, but that wasn't bad, he said, considering the day.

"Do you see any buzzards or hawks?" he asked suddenly.

I gulped, looked around and reported none.

He laughed at my apprehension. "They usually find thermals before we can," he said.

Feeling reassured, I considered the lazy circles of the birds, relaxing and enjoying the flight. The quietness was almost as soothing as my nap would have been.

"Want to fly it?" he asked.

"I guess so," I replied, snapping out of my reverie and taking hold of the stick as gingerly as if it were dynamite with a short fuse. Following Carl's instructions, I pushed on the pedals, used the stick and felt the glider go through a series of easy circles. I wasn't scared about the circles, but I worried about smashing up his glider.

"Hey, that was okay," he called. "You did it all by yourself for five minutes."

"Really?" I shouted so loudly they heard me on the ground.

"You did a great job," he said, taking over the controls, but letting me "follow through" on mine as we landed.

I was so busy getting the "feel" of the landing, I didn't have time to let go and wave at the boys, and I pretended not to hear later when they complained that all the clouds had dissipated by the time they went up. The other three soaring Sheetzes had to cut loose from the airplane, turn around and come back. My twenty-minute ride was the longest of the afternoon.

Carl deflated my happy bubble a little when he returned with Loren. "Mom is pretty good," he told the boys, "but you'd better stick with Dad. He's better."

Dad might be better, but I know who had the most fun—Carl. He says he would rather soar than fly or almost anything else. And I'd have to admit that, next to Sunday afternoon naps, he could be right.

And as a white-knuckle pilot and passenger who prays a lot when the engine coughs, I learned something my flight instructor and Loren had tried without success to convince me of—a craft doesn't really need an engine to land safely. Two wings and a good pilot are quite enough. It's the same reassurance we get when we give our lives over to the One who showed Peter he could walk on water, if he had faith. But, like Peter who panicked when he saw the winds, I have never soloed, even though everything I needed was there.

Gardening

When Loren's eyes glaze over, I know he's in the seed catalogs again. Along about February or March, nothing restores a man's faith in the future like a seed catalog in full color, and my winter-weary spouse is easily swayed by pictures of dwarf apple trees and burpless cucumbers.

It's a force known in the seed business as "the biological urge," the call to till the soil after a winter of snow and ice.

It's an urge so powerful I even find myself drooling over pictures of luscious, dew-covered vegetables, and even squash, which I detest, looks beautiful. The herbs sound fascinating, the celtuce, a vegetable used like celery or lettuce and loaded with vitamin C, looks interesting and so do the mangels, something I never heard of until the latest round of catalogs arrived. And there are banana muskmelons, onions shaped like torpedoes, corn that is avocado green and, would you believe it, a money plant.

Not only that, but you can buy dried blood to repel rabbits, field mice or deer and preying mantis eggs are only $2.49 for 900. Hatch your own. Gophers a problem? Try gopher gasser. It works wonders, according to the ads.

I'm always fascinated and a little skeptical by pictures of small boys pulling wagons completely filled by one gigantic tomato, but not enough to skip the ad.

"Do you think we could save much on the grocery bill if we had a garden this year?" Loren asked as he looked up from pictures of food.

"I read that one-third of the adult minimum daily protein requirement can be supplied by seven cents worth of lima beans."

"How much do you spend on lima beans a year?"

"About seven cents."

"That's what I thought," he sighed, his eyes still slightly glazed.

But it was a windy March night, and nothing would stay my desire to dream about a garden. Well, almost nothing. Having mentally ordered pecan trees, a mint garden, straw-

100

berry plants, even lima bean seeds and the money plant, I heard the wind bat the porch swing against the house. There was a horrible crash, and I gasped, "What was that?"

"You wouldn't believe me if I told you," Loren said. I hate him when he grins like that, like he knows something I don't. "Try me," I said, holding my finger on a picture of outdoor bamboo so I wouldn't lose my place.

"The wind just blew a jar with a live snake in it off the swing."

"Snake!" My finger slipped to thornless blackberries.

"Yeah," he said, disgustingly calm that even then a serpent lurked in the wild honeysuckle. "The boys found two this afternoon. They put one in a jar to take to school."

"Oh," I answered, quietly closing the catalog. If they could find two snakes in March, how many could I find under the lima beans in June — or in the bamboo or burpless cucumbers.

But dreams die hard, and soon I was out of the garden and into the lawn that would be velvety green, criss-crossed with walks of old brick and edged with beds of beautifully tended flowers, and I could see Loren was looking at ground cover that didn't have to be mowed.

It didn't matter that we weren't planting the same thing, because we both knew anticipation is worth more than an hour of gardening and if we had time to work outdoors, it would be spent battling the horseweeds and thistles that thrive so well among the rocks of Pucky Huddle.

If daydreaming about gardening is our only shared hobby, fighting the weeds that choked Pucky Huddle's first civilization is one of our shared battles.

Every state or country has its tree and flower, and Pucky Huddle's tree has to be the horseweed and its flower the thistle. I've even gone so far as to picture a flag with horseweed and thistle crossed against a field of stone. And I'm sure my tombstone will be from our fields and that our least favorite tree and flower will provide summer shade and winter thorns and stickers.

If a snake could make us quit dreaming about summer squash and tomatoes, so could it also remind us of those early dwellers of a perfect garden who were lured into sinning by a serpent. God told them that henceforth the soil would bring forth thorns and thistles. Jesus told us to plant our seed on good ground, and our answer is, "We're trying, but Adam and Eve sure messed up our chances of anything except pleasant dreams."

It's Contagious

When my hobbies threaten to become vices, Loren mutters, "This week I'm going to write 'Odds and Ends,'" implying it's high time someone "told on me" instead of my describing his or the boys' latest projects.

He said it most recently when I borrowed his truck to bring home a house. Not just any house, but a small, carefully detailed house constructed by someone with a lot of patience and a great deal of carpentry ability, a house certain to tickle the imagination of someone suffering from my particular affliction.

For reasons I have never fully understood, I'm a miniature nut. In a world gone wild by thinking big, I am intrigued by small things.

I have more tiny dishes and pieces of furniture than I did when I was eight, because then I hated everything even remotely "girl-like." The search for well-made items constructed on a one-inch to one-foot scale is a challenge I never tire of, and the fun of planning rooms for a miniature museum of my own helps put me to sleep at night. I recently spent a day at a miniature show where I was more excited than a cheerleader at a tied basketball game over a series of

102

rooms that included potting and florists' shops, a sewing room, a scene from "The Night Before Christmas" and so many others it took me days to quit talking.

Considering this, it wasn't strange that I should acquire the house, and it was unusual only because I had never before found one.

The really strange and unusual took place after Doug helped me carry the house into the kitchen. Clearly, he admired it every bit as much as I did, but Todd wrinkled his nose in distaste since it did not appear to be a moneymaker or in any way connected with farming. "I hope it was cheap," he said.

"It was," I assured him as I pointed out the solid construction, the detail in planning that included closets and space for stairs to a large attic.

His eyes got the same far-away look about them that Doug's and mine already had and he ran his hands over the solidly constructed rafters. "You know," he said, "if you went ahead and fixed this up, it'd be pretty tough."

"I thought we could put in windows and a fireplace," Doug said, pointing out a chimney made of hand-carved bricks.

By this time Loren had joined us. I expected him to laugh because, even to a confirmed miniature nut, the house in its present state is quite ugly. Instead, he checked the way the rafters are notched to fit over the plate, noted with satisfaction the space for a bathroom, kitchen, living room, dining room and two bedrooms. "A person could have a lot of fun with something like that," he said, admiring the tiny crosspieces that hold the floor joists apart. "We could set it on a table with an open top to give it the effect of having a basement."

The little house likewise mesmerized others. "Have you ever thought of wiring it?" a friend asked. We said we had

103

but did not know how. He found a way and later sent a sample light bulb no bigger than a baby's thumb nail.

"I can cut a neat opening in the roof and make stairs," Loren promises, and the boys think they can shingle the roof. All that remains for me is to devise a way to open the sides so I can get into the rooms to add walls and floors and to acquire skill to make furniture, since my collection is too large for the six-inch ceilings.

As we search for needed materials, it occurs to me that I'm not the only miniature nut in this house, and I wonder if the disease is contagious.

In the name of the One who healed instead of hobbying, but who recognized the value of going off by himself as we do when we lose ourselves in our hobbies, we give thanks for hobbies, the pause that restores after a hard day's or hard week's work. And we pray that the fact we belong to Christ can be as evident—and as contagious—to those with whom we associate as are our hobbies.

CHAPTER ELEVEN

...and Lives Together

Together

This is the story of four people who lived in the dining room.

It is not a tale of deprivation. We lacked nothing except mobility and for this we gave thanks. The rest of the time we counted.

The count started at forty-five and fifty-five. Wind speed, forty-five, oil level fifty-five gallons. Roads impassable. Only a ruffled bluejay moved in the swirling snow.

We'd talked about this before, and we all knew what to do. Loren closed the registers in the living room and den and the boys shut off the heat in the bedrooms. I gathered up our plants and moved them to the dining room while Loren hung a blanket over the door to the living room. Our nine-room house had been reduced to three.

By nightfall, the count was three, forty-five and ten. Three layers of clothes, forty-five gallons of oil and ten degrees in the living room, den and bedrooms. We wore coats when we went to those rooms for extra chairs and a portable television that picked up only one channel but formed our link with the world. I didn't have time to watch it because I was too busy cooking and washing—keeping the kitchen and utility room pipes thawed is how the eaters described it.

Still, cooking wasn't such a bad activity. It clearly beat

being in the dining room where the count was 45,000 and testy. A game of Monopoly between Loren and Doug had dragged on for two hours until my weary mate withdrew in favor of Todd, who was so restless he jumped at the chance to get in on the buying and selling. But he was more demanding than his father had been and rents were collected at the going rate and rules were followed to the letter.

By day's end, the snow was deeper, the winds just as strong and oil delivery day uncertain. Twin mattresses were moved to the dining room, but Todd and I declined, preferring our own rooms. He wore gloves and a sock cap. ("My nap cap," he said.) "I got along great," he reported later. His having the only electric blanket in the family may have had something to do with his comfort, but he didn't say. Hatless and with only a heating pad, I watched my breath freeze and felt frost form on the blankets. Within an hour I was chilled numb, eagerly seeking refuge with Loren and Doug on the dining room floor.

By morning my back throbbed and the count was three, thirty-five and ten. The thirty-five was most alarming and we dialed back to fifty-five and prepared to move the blanket to the kitchen door in the event the gauge wasn't right or we finally ran out of oil.

Telephone calls to my parents assured us they were fine, quite toasty, they said, and we envied them their electric heat and prayed the power didn't go off. But we didn't tell them about the close confines of our own living. "No need to worry them," we decided, knowing the eight miles that separated us might as well be eight thousand because of the drifts that completely covered fences and choked roads.

Every time we heard a noise, we raced to the window for some indication our solitude was ending, but we saw no one until Loren's brother arrived on a tractor to see how we

106

were doing. A look at the dining room told him. "Wonder if diesel fuel would work in your furnace?" he asked.

We didn't know, but we said we'd call the oil man to find out. He wasn't home and neither was his assistant, so we called my father, who until this winter had helped a cousin service winter heating customers. "Sure, it'll work fine," Dad said, and we bemoaned our silence, knowing we could have ended our worry days sooner if we'd only confided in the person who could help.

Loren and his brother hauled diesel fuel from his brother's tank in five gallon cans and we watched as the gauge rolled back to sixty-five, celebrating by cranking the thermostat to sixty-four and opening the register in our bedroom. The boys laid claim to the dining room, and we all slept soundly, for once not waking every thirty minutes to listen for the furnace.

Sunday dawned bright and beautiful. We were rested, the sun was shining and first one snowplow and then another led by a giant scoop cleared the roads past our house. No sooner had they moved on than we saw the most beautiful sight in the world sitting in our drive—an oil delivery truck with its hose in our fill pipe. I cried.

"You guys were good company, but I'm glad to be rid of you," I told my family as mobility loomed. "Same to you," they replied as they tore down the blanket, opened the registers and helped me carry the plants back.

We'll remember the long weekend as one in which we learned we could live in a lot less space than normal, developed increased admiration for the Amish and their way of life that is not dependent on man's systems but on the fuel supplied by God, and thought more about solar and wind power than before. And realized we'd never really known the meaning of cabin fever, a malady that in our instance broke on Monday when three vehicles rolled out of the drive in convoy formation to seek other roads that were open. Roads that would lead us back to work and direct communication with the outside world we'd found we could not live without.

Magnetic Sink

You can make electricity by stroking a cat, and Boy Scouts are told you can start fires by rubbing two sticks together. But I'm the only person in our family who can make a sink magnetic.

It's not difficult. In fact, it's more difficult not to do it.

All I have to do is fill the sink with water to wash dishes or scrub vegetables and suddenly I'm the most popular person in the world. My family materializes as if by magic, surrounding me completely. Except they don't really want to see me, they want a drink. The magnetic sink has done it again.

Perhaps the sound of waters draws them, I conclude, and change my habits.

It's 10 P.M. and the house is quiet. My mate is burning midnight oil at the shop, our sons are in bed. But, I discover as soon as the sink is filled, being in bed and being asleep are not the same. An outstretched hand holding a glass shows the sink has lost none of its magnetism.

It's late at night and my men are working in the field, trying to beat a rain. The house is strangely silent and I put off washing pots and pans in favor of a chance to read in peace and quiet. At 11 or 12 or 1, my conscience bothers me, and I move to the sink. Within seconds the hand is there.

I would attempt to patent my magnetic sink but there's no demand for it. The women of the world would pay more for one that is less magnetic, unless I can create one that brings a hand carrying a towel instead of a glass.

108

Demarcation Line

"Hmpf," Doug said, indignant as only a ten-year-old can get. "Anyone who says peeling apples is hard is crazy. There's nothing to it."

"Why are you sitting on the cupboard?" I asked in horror as I watched him slash apples with the same strokes he uses to sharpen sticks for wiener roasts.

"More comfortable this way," he said, wiggling into a new position that made his feet stick straight out in front of him and put the apples three feet from either arm.

Just looking at him made my back ache, but, even more, my whole person ached. Sharing the joys and work of cooking does not come easily for me, because, basically, I'm a loner. Oh, I let the boys empty trash and occasionally make popcorn, but I would no more think of sharing my kitchen with them—or anyone—than I would of sharing my husband or my toothbrush. For years there has been an imaginary demarcation line through the room. That side is Mom's. It's safe to be in the kitchen if you don't cross the line. That way Loren can "keep me company" while he drinks coffee and reads or the boys can do homework at the table, but no one gets between the sink, stove and refrigerator except me.

But—and there's always a big, qualitative but to everything—sometimes there have to be exceptions, and most of our exceptions are dictated by our stomachs. We aren't strong on packaged foods; we like homemade—from scratch. Being a working mother (that's a bad term, because we all work, but some of us also go out of the house to do it), makes it hard to have time for such favorites as apple cake or chop suey or any other dish that takes as long to chop ingredients for as it does to make. The only obvious solution is to let down the barrier and draft help. They can chop dates, nuts or onions at the table, but apples should be rinsed and I have to let them encroach on my territory.

"How many of these things do you need?" Doug asked cheerfully, visions of warm apple dumplings. dancing in his mind.

"I don't know," I admitted. "The recipe says to core an apple for each dumpling, but I like slices better so make four cups."

"Okay," he said, his enthusiasm waning as he noted the slices were still at the cup-and-a-half level.

I turned my back on the mess at the sink and rolled dough into a thin sheet and cut it.

The apples, finally ready, were deposited on the crust, and they seemed to swell. We had far too many.

"All my hard work and you're not going to use them," he grumbled.

"I'm sorry," I apologized as I sprinkled cinnamon sugar on the slices.

"What are you going to do with the leftover sugar?"

"Leave it in the shaker and put it back in the cupboard."

Looking from the apple slices to the sugar, he asked, "Do you like to throw out leftovers?"

"Not if I can help it. I always think about all the starving children in the world.

"Me too," he said, taking a spoon, the apples and sugar to the table where Loren joined him with a cup of coffee.

Sprinkling sugar liberally over the apples, he stuffed his mouth full and told his father, "That was a lot of work to get those apples sliced, and she didn't even use them all."

"So?" Loren teased, "you're getting to eat them, aren't you?"

"Just helping a starving child," Doug said, savoring the smell of cinnamon as he popped in the last bite before tip toeing back across the line to peek at the dumplings in the oven. They suited him, and he went back to the table. His job on the other side of the line was done.

110

In the name of the one who drew no demarcation lines, we pray for guidance in living, playing and sharing together. And we pray we may remember the wisdom of Ecclesiastes: "Woe to him who is alone when he falls and has not another to lift him up." How fortunate we are to have each other, but may we never forget there are some things, like diesel fuel, that call for outside help.

CHAPTER TWELVE

Reading, Writing and Balls for Science

Balls for Science

"You're wrong," Todd said, facing his father across the supper table. "The ball got there first."

"No way," Loren replied. "The dog got there first. It was heavier than the ball."

"It doesn't make any difference which was heavier, the ball fell first; it would beat the dog," Todd replied.

"Hey, Mom, tell me that story again," Doug whispered, and they all fell silent, evidently thinking a retelling of the gruesome tale would end the argument.

"A man wanted a date with a top New York model," I recited from a magazine article. "For months he asked a friend of his to arrange one. Finally, the big night came. He went to the girl's apartment, which was on the twelfth floor of an old building, and while he waited for her, he played with her dog, a Great Dane that weighed 200 pounds. He threw a ball and the dog returned it. The man threw it again, but the ball bounced on the floor and out an open window. To his horror, the Great Dane went right after it. He couldn't bring himself to tell the girl but he worried so much about the dog that the evening was ruined. In fact, he was sick twice, just thinking of the accident. The girl was furious, not knowing her dog was gone but thinking she had dated an absolute dud."

"You mean the dog fell the whole twelve stories?" Doug asked, and I nodded. It was a sickening story, and I was sorry I had mentioned it.

"Why don't we drop some stuff out an upstairs window?" he asked with nine-year-old logic as he faced his 15-year-old brother and his father. "That would solve the problem."

"What is there to solve?" I asked. "The dog is dead. I kept hoping he had fallen on a roof or an awning or something. He didn't. Somewhere, he and the ball scared the daylights out of some innocent bystanders."

"Still, we don't know," they said.

"The first one of you who takes Herkimer upstairs and tosses him out a window leaves home," I said, glaring at the three of them.

"Calm down," they said. "He doesn't weigh 200 pounds and, besides, you won't let us bring him in the house."

By the next morning, a strange assortment of balls had been assembled. There were softballs and nerf balls, the same size but much different in weight. There were baseballs and golfballs. And there were three oddballs, one of whom went to the attic and dropped the other balls to the ground crew. I watched from the warmth of the den as balls swished past the window, each heralded with a cheer from either a ground person or the man in the attic. Herkimer, taking no chances, did not share the excitement, preferring to peek through the hedge as the balls fell. I almost joined him when they started throwing balls back to the man in the window for re-runs of particularly close races.

Lacking a 200 pound, four-legged object and the proper distance, the argument did not end with the ball drop but continues to this day. I suppose I should cheer their scientific inclinations, but instead I find myself thinking of that poor dog and of the friend's reply when the man asked him what he should have done. "When she asked you if you'd

113

seen her dog, you should have said you had but you thought he seemed rather depressed," he said.

Depressed or not, he is probably the only one who knows which got there first, him or the ball. May he rest in peace with that knowledge.

X Times Y

I've always figured if God had intended us to be mathematicians he would have created us by formula instead of love, and if he had intended us to delve deeper into its mysteries, he would have given us built-in calculators instead of fingers and brains.

"Algebra looks like a dumb subject," Doug said as he watched Todd solve a problem that involved so many symbols it looked like something left over from one of Einstein's problems.

I wanted to grab the boy and hug him. Here was a lad after my own heart—one who recognized the true worthlessness of the subject. But, as usual, I was trapped. After all, here was one boy deeply involved in the subject, loving every minute of it, and another who would be ready to fathom its mysteries in a few years.

"It's not so bad," Todd said, looking to me for support.

"Well, it's different," I muttered. I remembered those agonizing years I grappled with math, hating every minute of it, much as they dislike spelling and English. I prayed God would forgive me as I gulped and said, "Algebra helps you figure out something you don't know."

"I don't know how to read German," Doug said. "Will it help me figure out what that book says?" he asked, pointing to a small volume written entirely in German script.

"It wouldn't help a bit," I said. "It helps you get the answer to number problems. For instance, you know two and two make four. If I say 2 plus X equals 4, what would X equal?"

He thought a minute and answered, "Two?"

114

"Right," I said, hoping he would change the subject.

"Gimme a harder one."

"That's the only one I know. You think of a number you'd like to know and your father will help you make an equation."

"How old are you?"

"She's four times as old as you are," Loren said.

"And you're seven," I teased.

"No, I'm not," he mumbled, chewing a pencil as he thought.

"She's two and one-half times as old as I am," Todd said.

"Which way is easier?" Doug asked. He had been ready with an answer; now he was confused.

"Either way's about the same," I said, adding, "do you remember when I was six times as old as you, three times as old as Todd and he was twice as old as you?"

"That wasn't very long ago, was it?" Todd asked.

"Be quiet, I'm figuring," Doug said, writing "six times three equals X." "X equals eighteen," he said. "You're eighteen."

"Good job," I said, patting him on the back and trying not to look at Todd or Loren. "Go get the German book," I whispered. "We'll see if we can figure it out the same way."

Get the Rule Book

"And whatever you do, don't forget to try to get a rule book," Loren yelled as I dashed out of the house. It was parents' night at school, and I was the only one free to go. My spouse was mired in a fifth grade mathematics book. His condition looked terminal.

For anyone who has not seen a fifth grade math book for thirty years and who remembers the subject as arithmetic, which the dictionary defines as the most basic form of mathematics, or who remembers how to spell it from the acronym, "A rat in the house might eat the ice cream," is going to be shocked when he opens a current textbook.

No longer is the subject taught by rote. Our flashcard drill sessions, even our struggles with fractions and long division, look like child's play compared to the basic principles for whole numbers.

There is the 0 principle: $34 + 0 = n$, and the 1 principle: $53 \times 1 = n$, but there is also the commutative principle: $5 \times n = 7 \times 5$ or $49 \times 51 = n \times 49$ and the associative principle $+$: $(5 + 2) + 3 = 5 + (2 + n)$ and the associative principle $\times$: $(n \times 3) \times 4 = 2 \times (3 \times 4)$. When they master this, they study the distributive principle: $6 \times 5 = 6 \times (3 + 2) = (6 \times 3) = (6 \times 2)$.

By the time they reach this plateau, they have already passed through something called the landing point: 7 (three in circle with right arrow and five in circle, also right arrow: give landing point).

And they have learned about function rules. One problem: Suppose the function rule on each machine is $f(n) = n + 9$. Write a multiplication equation that helps you find the output number for each machine.

Whether you call it math or arithmetic, it's not my favorite subject. In fact, it's pretty much accepted around here that when the Creator said math, I thought he said path and took a long walk. Which explains why, when the boys started to school, Loren and I agreed I would help them with languages and related subjects and he would concentrate on mathematics. It was a happy solution, one that helped Todd graduate from basic arithmetic through algebra and geometry, but we were totally unprepared for Doug's fifth grade mathematics.

I sympathized with Loren, offering him whatever assistance I could give.

"Just get a book," he pleaded, rereading: "There are only four whole numbers that can be used as input numbers in

116

the function rule f(n) = 27 ÷ n to give an output number that is a whole number. List the four number pairs that would appear on the input-output cards for this function rule."

My heart bled for him, and I rushed to school where I waited behind twenty other parents, all of whom were muttering "function rules" so loudly it sounded like a cheer at a pep rally. Unfortunately, there were no books for parents, but there was the encouraging news that all the fathers had been stumped by f(n) = 27 ÷ n, list four number pairs. It was encouraging to know ours was not the only family stymied by a fifth grade math book.

Encouraging but not very helpful. If it was that difficult on page 39, what would it be like by page 300? We turned the pages with bated breath and saw something that looked familiar: "⅝ of the children are girls. One-half of the girls went to the library. What part of the children went to the library?" But on the next page was another of our nemeses: ½ × 7 = n. But when we flipped to page 330, we found 356 − 163 = ? It looked promising, but on page 33, the problem was 5 × 5 × 5 × 5 = n.

I was glad I had taken that walk. I figured I'd need the strength, because, as Loren said, "If it's like this in fifth grade, God help us all in the sixth grade."

Meanest Teacher

A teacher who has replaced spankings, scoldings and other more common forms of punishment with strong doses of tender loving care came to visit my office one day. By the time she left Doug had declared her the meanest teacher in the state.

It'd been a year since we'd seen her, and there was the usual reminiscing and small talk. She and Doug, both antique enthusiasts, exchanged auction tidbits. A soon-to-be seventh grader, he didn't flinch when she said she taught seventh grade language arts, certainly not his favorite subject. A person who loves antiques could be forgiven a few things. And he limited himself only to an indulgent that's-just-like-a-mother smile when I asked, "Do you have many discipline problems?"

"Not this year," she said.

"What was different this year?" Doug asked, fascinated in spite of himself.

"The first day of school, our principal met with all the teachers. He told us we were to love all the children even if they were dirty, even if they disrupted class or had trouble concentrating. No matter what they did, we were to love them."

"That sounds okay," he said. Minutes before, he'd been bored at the prospect of spending the afternoon in the office. Now, he was intrigued.

"Do you like teachers who shout at you?" she asked.

"I hate them."

"So do I," she said. "And I decided the principal was right; I should love all my children." Looking at my son slouched over a typewriter, his feet wound around the casters of a chair, she continued, "So if one of the boys in my class gets a little noisy, I just go up to him and put my arm around him and say sweetly, 'Are you having trouble? You're making so much noise you must want my attention. I'm here. Now what is it you want?' "

"Right in front of the rest of the class?" Doug gasped.

"Right in front of everyone."

"Wow!"

"And if they're really naughty, I walk up to them and go like this," she said, advancing toward him with her lips puckered and a come-here wag of her finger.

"Oh no you don't," he yelled, unwrapping his feet and rolling a hasty retreat.

118

"What's wrong with getting kissed?"

"Look at all those people out there," he said, pointing to the window. "It wouldn't be so bad if there weren't people there. They'd see you."

"That's what the kids in class think, too," she said. "I may have kissed one boy three or four times this year, but I never had to do anything else. Or kiss him again."

"You never had to send anyone to the principal's office?" Doug asked, astonished.

"None," she said, laughing. "My husband is head custodian in the school. He saw the class bully in the hall one day and he asked him how he got along in my class. The boy answered sullenly, 'Just fine. She puts on fresh lipstick every day just before our class, and I sure don't want any of that stuff on me.' "

"For somebody that nice, she's sure one mean teacher," Doug said later, his face still pale at the thought of getting kissed in public.

"I thought the idea sounded great," I said. "Love instead of fear."

"Mom," he said in exasperation. "You just don't understand. She's got to be the meanest teacher in the state."

But in the name of the One whose disciples called him Teacher, I gave thanks for such a teacher. And asked God to grant us strength to help our children with their homework and the sense to love as we grope with the intricacies of mathematics and a road not always easy, one sometimes strewn with such small things as n factors and balls for science.

CHAPTER THIRTEEN

Cause for Celebration

Whatever its origin, almost any holiday is cause for celebration.

New Year's Resolutions

I keep New Year's resolutions longer than anyone I know—and most of them are just as good now as when I made them eight or nine years ago.

I figure I owe this skill to organization and to a husband who each year gives me a whopping big, elegantly clean one-year diary. "You're too wordy for a five-year one," he said when he gave me the first big journal and watched with amusement as I fingered its pages with reverence. Some women go bananas in dress shops; I get slightly intoxicated just looking in a stationer's window. I love paper, and all those clean pages left me breathless.

When the new year dawned, I opened the crisp pages carefully and in my neatest handwriting sketched in my year's goals. I'd long ago promised to give up resolutions in favor of goals, and it's been the easiest resolution in the world to keep, because a goal lets you work towards it instead of demanding that you keep it.

And who can fault a goal like breathe deeply—outdoors? Certainly not I, and I'm sure I've done it at least once a year since I first entered it.

And what's wrong with trying to eat properly? It doesn't

120

demand that I lose weight or give up forever butter brickle ice cream spread on coconut cookies; it merely asks that I try to eat properly. A good goal.

A nice healthy group, my goals. They fill the entire front page of my diary.

A funny thing happened this year when I copied the list. I don't know if I actually became better organized or if I wrote smaller, but there was an extra line at the bottom and I used it to record the closest thing to a resolution I made: Become more like the Shakers.

I liked the line so well I read it to my family.

"How do you figure?" Doug asked.

"The Shakers had a theory that less is more."

"So?"

"So less eating means more new clothes. Less spending means more savings."

"I don't like it," said the boy whose main interest in life is his workshop. "Sooner or later, you're going to say less tools for me means more milk for the kids in Pakistan or India."

"Could be," I teased as I served our annual New Year's dinner of sauerkraut and hot dogs.

He was silent for a few minutes. "You know," he said between bites, "you could be right. If Dad spent less for your diaries, you'd get more years in one book and you'd have less space to put in dumb things like that and more time to fix something good to eat. Less sauerkraut could mean more apple crisp. Less talk could mean more action."

The kid catches on quickly. In another year or two I'll have to get him a diary of his own — maybe a ten-year one. Just because he's at the age of resolution doesn't mean he is ready for unlimited goal-making. One Shaker in the family is enough; the rest had better be movers.

Lent

I gave up sweet and salty snacks and seconds for Lent.

Our church doesn't require that we give up anything; I just wanted to do something constructive, something that hurt a little, and denying myself food was as painful as anything I could think of, even if the selfish side of me knew that losing a few pounds wouldn't be much of a sacrifice.

And so, instead of seconds, I simply ate bigger first helpings and, instead of sweet and salty snacks, I drank a lot of tea and ate apples. But then came the final week of Lent, the one that is the saddest of all weeks, the one that began locally with rain, fog and general gloom, and the devil hit me where I am weakest — with an attack of chocoholism that could be treated only with a bag of chocolate-covered peanut clusters.

Washing down the last of the chocolate with cups of hot tea, I stared out my office window at the bulletin board on the church lawn across the street and read: "The values of Lent are not based in what we give up but what we take up."

I felt a little better because I knew I had given up one thing — a few hours of time for a prayer experiment group that had become one of the most meaningful experiences of my life, one in which I'd become closer to many people I had known, but not really known, all my life. It was a giving that resulted in my getting more than I gave.

I reflected on the prayer group, on the experiences we had shared and on our answered and unanswered prayers. And I thought again of the week that always seems so sad, that this year began with rain and gloom, that would end, as always, with the saddest day in Christendom — Good Friday. And I began to cry, which isn't unusual, except these were tears of joy at a Good Friday story with a happy ending, a prayer dramatically answered.

The narrator was a woman whose husband was a minister. They lived full and active lives, but there had been a time during World War II when life had not been so happy. Her

122

husband had been a prisoner of war. The men prayed for release, but days turned into weeks and months and it seemed they were destined to spend the rest of their lives in prison, their prayers unanswered.

"By the time Good Friday came," she recalled, "morale was at rock bottom."

"Then, just at the time Christ was suffering on the cross, there came a loud roar and General Patton's tanks knocked down the gates of the prison and the men were freed."

Talk about answered prayer, that was real in a way more vivid than most of us will ever experience.

Remembering the men's misery, I wept at my weakness. I looked again at the bulletin board and wondered if it wasn't about time I took up something more positive than chocolate binges, something like tank driving maybe. And it was then in that gloomy moment that the real power of our prayer group hit me, and I realized we were all, in effect, learning to be tank drivers. And some of us, by our own making, were prisoners too blinded by the present to see the joy and promise that mark the end of this sad week— Easter.

And I wasn't thinking about chocolate bunnies and marshmallow eggs.

Mother's Day

In a few weeks it will be Mother's Day, my nineteenth as both mother and daughter, but chances are it will be nothing like the first, the one we spent tramping around graveyards in Luxembourg. Luxembourg, I should explain, is the native land of my maternal grandparents. Centuries removed from the paternal ancestors whose migration paths have long been obscured, I found it rewarding to trace my roots in a place where some of the people actually remembered my relatives. But forays through local cemeteries were less fruitful and we ended our day in a camp spot on a hill, tired and frustrated.

As we unloaded our borrowed camping gear, the loneliness of being separated from Todd, then a three-month-old charmer staying with friends in Germany, caught up with me. I swallowed a lump and said, "Here it is, my first Mother's Day, and I'm not with my baby." I reached for a dry tissue and knocked the tent over.

The idea of having to set up the tent again didn't appeal to Loren, but the prospect of me mooning around appealed even less. He handed me a bucket and said, "Go back to the restaurant where we checked in and get some water."

Alternately thinking of Todd and the thrill of actually being in the country I had heard so much about from my grandmother, I followed Loren's instructions. Go to the restaurant, he had said. I did. And found myself standing in the middle of an elegant eating establishment holding a bucket, praying none of the diners were distant cousins. Being the only person in the room who spoke English didn't help much, but, finally, after a great show of arm waving by both the waitress and myself, I was directed "around the corner."

Now intently alert, I went around the corner and saw a door labeled "Filles." I knew that meant "ladies" so I went in and was filling my pail at a basin when a German woman came in and followed my example. Carefully trying our knowledge of the other's language, we hadn't advanced very far when her husband, who obviously watched her more closely than mine did, burst into that ladies-only confine. I'm not sure what he said, and it's probably just as well. He jerked both buckets out of the basins and led us around another corner to a faucet.

Like much of life, it was so simple, once we found the right corner.

"What's new at the restaurant?" Loren asked when I rejoined him.

"Not much," I answered. How do you explain something like that? The hour was getting late and after a light supper, we turned in for the night. He fell asleep immediately while I lay awake thinking about being a mother.

Suddenly the still night was filled with banjo music and giggles. And then there was a horrible racket as an animal scampered across our tent. Loren was dead to the world while I sat up in my sleeping bag, paralyzed with fright, thinking how stupid I was to be there on Mother's Day, of all days, and wishing I were in Germany with Todd.

In the morning, we learned a honeymooning couple had camped next to us. He had serenaded her with banjo music and she had giggled her applause. The noise had awakened a cat that picked that time to fight with another camper's dog, and they had chosen our tent for their pitched battle. Muddy paw prints indicated the cat had found refuge on top of the tent but the dog had not given up easily.

There's no doubt about it. Sunday's family dinner, with two boys instead of one, church and all the other activities, will lack something if we compare it to the first. But the same love will be there, in abundance.

Proverbs says, "She that bore you shall rejoice," and I will. Twice blest, every day is Mother's Day and a day for rejoicing. Some more than others.

Whatever Happened to Thanksgiving?

If it hadn't been such an absolutely perfect fall day, there is no way Halloween would have started at our house on the third of October. As it was, it had been a day with sky so clear visibility was unlimited. Only a poet could have described the blueness; red fingers of an early sunset added more beauty. It was crisp and cold; the leaves had not yet

125

begun to fall, but the feeling of autumn was in the air. It made you feel good just to be alive, and it made me an absolute pushover for an eager eight-year-old who said, "Hey, Mom, how about getting some pumpkins for Halloween?"

It didn't take long to select two big pumpkins and it didn't take much longer to whittle out two ugly jack-o-lanterns with leering grins and corn cob pipes. I smiled complacently as they were carried to the front porch, but suddenly, instead of seeing pumpkins I was seeing a Christmas tree put up on the third of December that had no needles by December 20. "Don't light them," I ordered.

"Why not?"

"Because," I faltered. They couldn't lose needles, could they? "Because they'll shrivel and won't look good for Halloween," I said. "Besides, who ever heard of jack-o-lanterns a month before Halloween?

"Lots of kids, I'll bet."

"Do something else."

"Phooey," he grumbled, but within a few days he had constructed twin scarecrows that he tied to the porch posts. Their own gourd heads quickly shrunk until the twins looked headless except for the grinning jack-o-lanterns beside them.

And those jack-o-lanterns were a fright. Rain, snow and fog had followed the one perfect day, and each took its toll. The heads were definitely flabby. By Halloween they would be soft enough to use for putty.

The condition was not unnoticed by the eight-year-old. "How long until Halloween?" he asked so often I showed him the calendar and told him to keep track of his own time.

He was so silent I worried about him, but when I checked I found him curled up in a chair with a notebook and pencil. "Bless his heart," I sighed. "He's going to be a writer."

126

Hours later, he presented me with pages and pages of penciled notes. "Here, Mom," he said. "I made out my Christmas list. The things I couldn't spell, I circled in catalogs. You should find everything there you want to get me."

He went back to check the pumpkins, leaving me holding the list and wondering whatever happened to Thanksgiving and hoping it didn't snow on the third day of December.

CHAPTER FOURTEEN

'Tis the Season

The celebration of Jesus' birth and the old German festival of the winter solstice with its yule logs and evergreens have been intertwined so long we seldom think of one without the other. Some sects do not celebrate Christmas at all, saying it is merely a pagan observance that has nothing to do with Christ's nativity, but others of us enter into the festival with joy, anticipation and sometimes frustration. Occasionally we stop to ask, "Whatever happened to the old-fashioned Christmases we used to know?" And, of course, we have only to look to ourselves to find the answer.

In this collection of Christmas "Odds and Ends," the only chronological chapter in this book, I can see what has happened to Christmas in the Sheetz family, and I do not like the changes our getting older has created. The love is still there, but the anticipation has given way to practicality, and the excitement is subdued, possibly because we no longer have a pre-schooler searching for the right gift for an invisible family. . . .

A Gift for Joe Mere

The tree is up and the boys have begun rising before dawn to watch it, plans for family dinners have been made and most of the shopping is done. If we had gifts for Joe Mere, his wife Ruth and their son Board, we would be about ready for Christmas, but it's not that easy. Joe Mere and his family have almost everything. Or so we are told. No one knows them except four-year-old Doug.

Joe Mere does no wrong. In Doug's mind, he is as nearly perfect as it is possible for a mortal to be. A busy farmer who keeps an immaculate barn, Joe Mere has time to be a member of the school board and take his son with the improbable name of Board to kindergarten in his new dump truck.

Ruth Joe Mere (the name is both first and last) has a house full of new appliances and makes candy most of the time. She also excels at cooking and baking—mostly cakes, pie, cookies and doughnuts. Ruth and Joe Mere let Board eat as much or as little of anything as he wants, mostly candy and cake. However, Board is a good kindergarten student, although Ruth and Joe Mere don't make him go if he doesn't want to.

Board has rooms full of toys and is allowed to play with them all night if he so desires. The list of things and privileges already possessed by Board is endless.

We'd like to suggest a little more discipline and some regular eating habits for Board, but that's not what Doug has in mind. He feels you can't improve on perfection and when you have everything going for you, like Ruth and Joe Mere and Board have, there is little left to suggest. So you can see what problem is slowing Christmas this year.

Family Christmas

Some families make rare occasions out of trimming the Christmas tree. If they don't have a party, they at least join in singing carols and drinking hot chocolate. Not our family. Not only can't we sing, if we haven't killed each other by the time the tree's up we're ready to put arsenic in the hot chocolate. The togetherness of putting up a tree leaves our nerves ragged and frayed, our tempers belying the true spirit of Christmas.

The trouble is, we're all individuals. Loren is a perfectionist. Every light has to be properly spaced, no two ornaments of the same size or color can hang near each other. Each decoration must be in perfect condition. Todd is a sentimentalist. Nothing should be thrown away and nothing should be changed. Doug is a saver. Nothing is ever thrown away. Junk comes out of the trash barrel faster than it goes in. All of this conflicts with a mother who is basically a loner, who likes to work by herself and get lost in thought, an attitude that does not relate well to a gregarious family that not only fights together but talks loudly while doing it.

We solved the problem this year. I threw them all out. Lock, stock and boots, they were lined up and marched out the door while I tackled the business of tree trimming alone.

"Why does Doug save everything?" I moaned as I dusted some beautiful ornaments I'd rescued from the trash. Why would anyone throw away a perfectly good decoration that was only dirty?

"Why is Todd so sentimental?" I asked as I put in place the delicate snowflakes cut from paper that a pen pal sent Loren years ago, and carefully hung a decorated egg she sent another time. Take care of the glass church, I reminded myself, remembering the shopping trip in Germany that resulted in so many gay ornaments we cherished, the church most of all.

"Why can't he ever let us change anything?" I growled as I scooted around the floor hanging the styrofoam decorations we've always used on the bottom.

"What's so sentimental about Christmas trees?" I asked, remembering an uncle who had loved the only really big tree we ever had so much he looked at it over and over,

130

repeating, "That's the prettiest tree I ever saw." It was his last Christmas with us.

We remembered the year Loren's father died five days before Christmas, and how we consoled the boys by telling them God had wanted him to spend the holidays in heaven with Grandma. But our own hearts were so heavy that there had been no new decorations and little joy. To help things out I added tiny doves to our tree and prayed for the peace they represented.

Three hours sped by so rapidly I barely realized the thousands of trips up and down the ladder as the decorations fell in place. The aloneness was wonderful. I felt completely renewed, and the tree was beautiful when the men in my life came in for hot chocolate. They reported they had cleaned the barn to perfection. Todd had driven the tractor, a first he insisted he'd remember all his life. Doug, who had already sorted the trash barrel, picked through broken decorations I'd discarded and agreed the tree looked wonderful.

And it is a wonderful tree, one we've all enjoyed for not having argued while we put it up. We each got to do something our own way. In doing it we came to a better understanding of each other than enforced togetherness would ever have allowed. We may even try singing one of these nights.

Maybe He'll Reorder

Last Christmas was disappointing for Doug. Although he was only five, he knew what he wanted and he ordered carefully. The only problem was that Santa Claus was unable to fill his order with the right model and make of tractor and, while he enjoyed the substitute, he has been a little dissatisfied with Santa all year.

Now a year older, a first grader with one missing tooth

131

and another ready to fall out, our little warrior has been intent on this year's list. We should have noticed not as much was said about Santa bringing the goodies this year, but the rush of the season has already affected our listening abilities, and it took a minute for the seriousness of the situation to be felt one night last week when he seemed to retreat within himself. Finally, he mustered his courage and in a firm tone said, "Mom, there's something I want to know and I want you to tell me the truth." About six dozen possibilities rushed through my mind, and most of them were bad. I braced myself.

"Is there really such a person as Santa Claus?"

If I hadn't been driving, I think I would have scooped him into my arms and cried. Instead, I swallowed hard and answered, "There is if you want to believe it." I explained the old myths and said yes, it was true, mothers and fathers bought the presents, but if you really truly wanted to believe, Santa was real. "The main thing to remember, though, is that Christmas is not just for Santa Claus but a celebration of the birth of Jesus, God's greatest gift to us."

Silence accompanied a saddened mother and a troubled little boy the rest of the way home. My plans for baking Christmas cookies that night almost vanished in the quiet of the crisis, but as I talked myself out of the mood and gathered the ingredients, a soft voice at my elbow whispered, "I think I do believe, Mom. I think that's what God wants me to do."

"That's fine, Doug. If you want to believe that, Santa is really real."

He gave me a hug and a kiss. It was a precious moment and it seemed like a good time to explain about the tractor. "You see, Doug, since parents are really Santa Claus, sometimes they just cannot find or afford the exact toy you boys order. That's the reason Santa got the order mixed up on the toy tractor last year."

"By golly, that's right," he replied, the magic moment

132

shattered in the wake of this new discovery. "I wonder if he'll be able to get the right model this year," he said as he swiped a handful of dates and fled.

If he only knew! Santa hasn't the vaguest idea what kind of tractor he had in mind. We hope he plans to reorder.

A Democratical Vote

"It would be more democratical if we voted," Doug said.

I started to say, "You mean more democratic, don't you," but I was interrupted by Todd, who asked incredulously, "You mean you want us to vote where to put the Christmas tree?"

"Sure, why not?"

"You put it in the living room and I'm not going to pick needles out of the carpet," Todd warned. "Put it in the dining room."

"What do you think?" I asked Loren.

"Anything would be better than picking needles out of the carpet," he said.

Doug had located four slips of paper and a pencil. He turned to his father and asked, "Are you a Democrat or a Republican, Dad?"

"This is a referendum. You don't have to register party affiliation to vote in a referendum."

"How you gonna vote?" Doug demanded, ignoring the civics lesson.

"For the dining room."

"You're a Democrat. You'll have to wait," Doug said, turning to his brother. "How about you, Todd?"

"I always thought I was a Republican, but I guess I must be a Democrat," he said as he tried to take the pencil Doug refused to relinquish.

"You look like a Republican, Mom," he said, and I was given the honor of casting the first vote. He took his turn next and then reluctantly handed the pencil to his father and brother.

When the ballots were all in, he put them in his hat, swung it over his head and said, "Okay, Mom, pick out a slip."

"This isn't a lottery," I told him gently. "You have to take the ballots out and count them."

"Oh, you mean counting votes is democratical?" he asked, dumping the four slips of paper onto the table. "Okay, here's mine — it's for the living room. Here's another one for the living room and. . . ." His face fell as the two dining room votes were unfolded.

"Now what will we do?" he asked. "There are two votes for the dining room and two for the living room."

"You come home on the bus tonight and I'll come home from work early and we'll see what we can work out," I told him.

By the time Loren and Todd came home that evening, Doug and I were nearly finished decorating the tree. "I'm the underneath man," Doug called excitedly as he scooted around hanging ornaments in a tight circle against the trunk. The living room looked like a cyclone had struck.

"Well, so much for the 'democratical' process," Loren laughed.

"Hey, Dad," Todd exclaimed, "I thought we voted on this. Who broke the tie?"

"Herkimer," Doug said.

"How could that dog vote? He never even gets in the house."

"Just did, that's all," Doug said, adding a final ornament and rolling from under the tree.

"I see what you meant, Dad, when you told me that sometimes you vote for something but don't get it," Todd said as he picked up a book, ignoring the tree project completely.

134

I'd have to admit that wasn't a very "democratical" way to decide the tree's location, but Christmas comes only once a year, and if we really work at it, we can probably get all the needles picked up in time to vote again.

Every Day Is Christmas

"It's just not Christmas without a tree," Loren and I agreed when we were married, and no matter where we were, every year we had a gaily decorated pine that wafted its sweet smell and its sharp, pointy needles through the house.

It was a tradition we loved, but we found ourselves spending more and more holidays bickering over where the tree was to stand. By the time the boys were old enough to help pick needles out of the carpet, at least one of them always cast his vote with his father in favor of some room other than the living room.

"It's just not right," I would protest, and we would go into a long discussion about where that year's tree would be located, who had to pick up the needles and who should take which boy and run if the house burned down.

After one of those annual discussions, we decided the time had come to buy an artificial tree. Me, the woman who hates artificial, who can't stand plastic. I couldn't believe I'd gone along with the idea, but there it was—our first perfectly formed tree. And, I had to admit it didn't look bad. For once we had a tree that wasn't flat in the back, that didn't have lots of space between some branches and hardly any between others. It didn't smell as good, but when we took it down there wasn't much mess.

But there's the catch. We didn't take it down. Oh, we took the ornaments off, and Loren and the boys carried it to the attic where they draped it with a sheet of blue plastic film. None of this yearly hassle of which branch goes into which

135

hole for us. We'd have our tree intact come next Christmas. And we did, too. But it was there for the 4th of July, for Halloween, for the boys' birthdays. You name the date, and if you happened into our attic, you'd find a Christmas tree draped in blue plastic.

Somehow, by last Yule season, the idea of dragging a tree downstairs that had stood intact all year didn't seem very appealing, but we'd paid so much for the thing there was nothing else to do.

But it hadn't really ended the arguments. "Doggone it, Doug," I'd snap at our youngest, the only one still willing to help, "pull on that end of the lights. I know they'll straighten out. We didn't put them away tied in knots."

"Yeah, but that's the way they are now," he'd snarl, and Todd would yell, "Keep quiet!" By this time, Loren had either tuned us out or gone back to work. The tree had become a chore, a real grind.

Which is why I let myself be talked into putting it away with the lights still in place. If seeing a tree on the 4th of July had been disconcerting, seeing a tree complete with lights on the hottest day of the year was a bit much.

But there were other ways to fight. Doug and I carried the tree downstairs the other night, and I found myself yelling, "For heaven's sake, be careful, you've hooked the lights around the stair post."

"I didn't mean to," he said. I sighed.

"I said I didn't mean to," he repeated.

"There's nothing that says I can't sigh, is there?" I yelled, sighing again.

We stood the tree in the living room and I looked at it and sighed again. The branches drooped and the places where the lights had caught were pulled into odd little clumps. It had become a plastic hater's nightmare.

But a funny thing happened when we decorated the tree.

136

Oh yes, we decorated it, Doug and I. Mostly Doug, because I had so many other things I thought had to be done. But it looks kind of nice. The lights don't all work, but they never did. The ornaments pretty well cover the flat spot in the back, just like they used to, and if you don't look too closely, you can't see the bare spots between the branches.

And tonight, after I've sprayed the living room with a pine-scented aersol and dumped a handful of pine needles in the carpet, I aim to gather my family around and see if those shiny balls still have the same magical quality they did when I was seven and discovered that if you looked into them you could see forever.

And I have a feeling we'll be able to. There are some things about Christmas that are so constant arguments and plastic can't kill them, and the magic and wonder are but two.

We pray the One whose birthday started the whole thing will forgive us for the rest.

CHAPTER FIFTEEN

Nostalgia

How Can You Tell They're Old?

"**D**id you pick up the mail?" I asked Loren as he came into the kitchen.

"Completely forgot it."

"What's the matter? Getting old?" I teased as I rushed about preparing the evening meal.

"How do you know when someone's getting old?" eight-year-old Doug asked.

"What's for supper?" fourteen-year-old Todd asked as he raided the refrigerator.

"Pancakes and sausage."

"How do you know when someone is getting old?" Doug asked his father who was wearing a silly grin. Finally he burst out laughing. We all stared at him.

"Would you mind letting us in on the joke?" I demanded.

"I was just remembering the time you left a pancake on the griddle too long and when you threw it out for the dog, it stood up on edge and rolled down the drive like a cart-wheel with the dog right behind it."

"Wow, Mom! How'd you do that?" the boys asked in unison.

"Just lucky, I guess," I growled as I put the food on the table. "Some people remember the craziest things."

"I'll never forget it," Loren said, laughing so hard he spilled his coffee.

"Was that when you were young?" Doug asked.

"Did you remember to get some shoe strings?" Todd asked.

"Forgot all about them," I answered, "but one thing I'll never forget is the time your father broke your bed in the middle of the night."

"Was he young?" Doug asked.

"Real young," I replied. "They both were. Todd watched the Flintstones on television all the time and was always jumping from one thing to another yelling, 'Abba Dabba Do.' Well, anyway, as we went to bed, Todd sat up in his bed and said, 'Come kiss me goodnight, Daddy.' Your father got a good fast running start, yelled, 'Abba Dabba Do!' and jumped in bed with Todd. The next thing we knew, your father, Todd and most of the bed were on the floor and Todd was saying, 'Daddy, I just wanted a kiss. You didn't have to break my bed.' Doug, that had to be the funniest thing I ever saw in my life," I said, laughing so hard tears streaked across my face.

"Todd, do you know how to tell when a person is getting old?" Doug asked, obviously hoping to get more attention from his brother than he was from his parents.

"I'm not sure," Todd replied, looking from one of us to the other, "but I think it's when a person can't remember things in the present but can remember all the silly things that happened in the past."

Roses Are Red

"I love you little, I love you big. I love you like a little pig," I read.

"Yech! Is that gross. What is it?" Todd asked from his favorite prone position in front of television.

"That's what your dad wrote in my autograph book when we were in the fourth grade," I replied.

"An autograph book! What's that?"

139

"It's a book that everyone wrote greetings in," I said, waving the small book I had unearthed in a burst of spring cleaning.

"Any famous people in there?" Doug asked, taking the book from me.

"Sure. All our classmates are there."

He wasn't listing. "Wow! Dig this," he said, " 'Roses are red, violets are blue. Sugar is sweet and so are you.' Boy, is that dumb."

"Let's see that thing," Todd demanded, rolling into a semi-sitting position and holding his nose as he read, "May your heart be filled with sunshine, may your life be long and gay, until some nice little fellow says, 'Dearest, won't you name the day?' "

"Did they always write corny stuff?" they asked.

"Not at all. Listen to this. 'When your days on earth are ended and the path no more you trod, may your name in gold be written in the autograph book of God.' "

"Sounds like you were ready to die."

"She wouldn't have dared," Loren said, reading over my shoulder. "Not when there was someone writing, 'My pen is poor, my ink is pale, my love for you will never fail.' "

"That was my aunt, you dingaling."

"Well, that was no aunt who wrote, 'You're 2 sweet 2 be 4 gotten'."

"Wonder what ever happened to him?" I mused as I read, "When you get old and can't eat, take off your shoes and smell your feet."

"You're kidding!" Todd gasped.

"We weren't always kind," I answered, reading. "Roses are red, violets are blue, you've got a shape like a B-52."

That turned Todd off completely and he said, "Why don't you and Doug get away from in front of the TV?" We pretended not to hear.

140

"Let me see some more of that stuff," Doug said. "Hey! Here's a good one: 'Ann had a little cow and oh, how it did stutter. In place of milk, it gave a pound of butter.' "

"I've got a good one," Todd yelled. "Roses are red, violets are blue, sit down, you're blocking the view."

"Caught on rather quickly, didn't he?" Loren laughed as Doug and I moved out of the televiewing area.

"I don't think he's into this nostalgia thing very much," I said. "But thirty years from now when I find his Archie Bunker and 'Pigs Are Beautiful' sweat shirts, I'll wrap them around his recording of 'The Streak' and wait for the fun when his kids see all that stuff."

"The way fads run in cycles, they'll be too busy collecting autographs to pay any attention."

"Could be," I said absently. Already I was wondering whatever happened to that fellow who wrote, "You're 2 sweet 2 be 4 gotten." It was a lot more romantic than "I love you little, I love you big."

Oh well, no matter. If he loves me little and loves me big, that says it all. Besides, he could have said I had a shape like a B-52.

Rags

If it takes a heap of living to make a house a home, it takes twice as many rags to keep it operating.

"What'd you use before I outgrew my pajamas?" Doug asked as I washed windows.

"Your old diapers," I said, wondering if it would be considered frivolous to buy a dozen just for windows.

"Diapers on windows?"

"Best there is," I said, carefully turning the pajama top so the snaps wouldn't scratch the glass. It didn't seem possible my husky child had ever worn the tiny things. A lot of memories end up in rag bags.

141

Actually, we don't have a rag bag. We have a big, overflowing box that draws people to it, whether they are dripping blood, paint or mud.

But if there is a rag for every purpose, there is a purpose for every rag. No one but me is allowed the sheet blankets. They make soft dust cloths and work great for mops. Faded shirts and dresses make good paint rags, and for polishing shoes, nothing beats the corner of a holey towel. For sudden spills, it's often the first thing we grab, whether it's Dad's army shirt or Mom's retired maternity top. Worn blue jeans never make it to the rag box; they're cut up for patches for the next pair.

It's been a long time since I sewed "carpet rags" from discarded clothes, but I remember the fun that went into that winter project. It sometimes seemed sad to cut up aged garments without a little horseplay, which explains why our farm dog once greeted my father dressed in my shorts and my brother's old tee shirt. They later found their way into the rags, and we remembered the fabric both for the fun we'd had wearing the clothes and for Ginger's silly expression as she paraded around wagging her tail rather foolishly, afraid to sit for fear she'd pop a button on the shorts.

I haven't told the boys much about carpet rags and dressing dogs. Some things are better kept as memories, and they'll just have to remember the rag box we all work out of, knowing full well their dog would settle for nothing less than the jeans we can't spare.

"Forget the past", we are admonished. But how can we forget it when it is filled with love and joy overflowing in rag boxes and autograph books? Memories that bind us to each other and promises made to God, so that in living and remembering, we know all things work together for good, even memories of a time past when we were young and could yell "Yabba Dabba Do!"

142

CHAPTER SIXTEEN

Getting Away From It

Writer's Workshop

My family greeted with mixed emotions the news that I intended to spend a weekend at a writer's conference.

"It'll be good for you, sort of a vacation," Loren said. Translated, that meant he wanted to tear apart an old press and without me there to demand prompt meal times, he and the boys would be free to wade into the ink-soaked machine with abandon.

"What'll you do?" Todd asked.

"Learn to take better pictures, write better stories, be more creative. . . ."

"You gotta go to a conference for that? Can't you just try harder here?"

"Attend the governor's press conference, visit the statehouse, tour Indianapolis."

"Maybe you'll see a farm implement dealer," he said. "Be sure to leave a lot of snacks."

Doug was not as easily convinced. "You gonna be by yourself?"

"I'll drive carefully, keep my doors locked and the windows closed."

"Better tell the hotel not to take any calls for you except from your husband and boys."

"Don't worry," I assured him. "Nobody'll get me."

"Just remember," Loren reminded him, "we can tear apart that old press while she's gone."

"Yeah!" the boy answered, his face brightening at the prospect of the extra parts and pieces he could scavenge. "How soon you leaving, Mom?"

The weekend was all I'd hoped it would be; the sessions and tours were informative, the people I met intelligent, well-informed and highly creative. It was a heady experience, and I could hardly wait to share the excitement with my family.

A row of inky shoes and a pile of absolutely filthy clothes gave mute testimony that their weekend had been equally perfect. They were ready to hear about mine.

"What'd you do?" Todd asked.

"Learned to take better pictures, write better stories, be more creative. . . ."

"Gee, you mean you did everything they said you would?" he asked, his disappointment so obvious he didn't even ask about the farm machinery.

"Well, we didn't have any riots or anything like that."

"Did you meet the governor?"

"Not only did I meet the governor, I was on television."

That sounded more exciting. "How'd you do that?" they demanded, and I had to admit I'd only chanced to sit in the camera's range at the press conference.

"Didn't you have to sing or anything?" Doug asked.

I tried to change the subject. "I met a woman who had written 112 books."

"If you'd write even one book, you might be able to buy me a pair of cowboy boots," he said.

"Did you miss me?" I asked Loren, but he didn't hear. He was busy trying to get ink out of his hair and from under his fingernails.

"Sure, we missed you, Mom," Todd said. "But you could have stayed longer. We aren't out of snacks yet."

"It doesn't sound like you had any trouble," Doug said, "so I guess you could go again." Then, looking at his ink-soaked shoes, he added, "I think you'd better. Maybe you could learn to write a book because I sure could use some cowboy boots."

There's a Reason

There's a reason for this, I thought as I drove to an out-of-town meeting. My cold was better, the weather was perfect, traffic flowed easily. I didn't know what it was, but I knew as certainly as I knew God was alive and well that there was a reason for the trip.

"Great meeting," my friend Pat and I agreed as we walked to our room later. "There's a reason for our being here, you know," she said, and I nodded. We attributed it to the fact we'd decided to be practical and not drive back to our respective homes after dark. Let others battle the night. We had reserved a room and planned to be well rested for our own return trips.

Hours later, we switched off the lights. We'd talked of our work, our families, our goals. Now we were exhausted. "Wow! What made us talk so long?" I mumbled, settling into my bed.

"Dunno, but there's a reason," she said, pulling a pillow over her head.

Morning came and I leaped from bed at the sound of scraping outside the door. It was a man with a snow shovel. Tons of the white stuff blanketed the area. "What a bummer," Pat said, pulling the pillow over her head again. Editor of a monthly magazine, she had put it to press before she left. "I can coast the rest of the week," she said.

"Not me," I said. "This is my bookkeeping day. I have to

145

get back." I went to the lobby; the desk clerk reported all roads closed. I waded knee-high drifts in the parking lot to ask a policeman how the roads were.

"Just like this," he said.

I went back to the lobby. "Can we go south?" a young mother asked another policeman.

"How far south?"

"Florida."

He stared at her, and she settled the children on the floor with books. "There's a reason for this," she said.

Pat and I went to the coffee shop. If we couldn't leave, we would eat. "I'll take a whole pot of coffee," a woman at the next table said, and the waitress laughed. "I mean it," the woman said as she turned to us. "The roads are horrible."

By the time we left we had consumed gallons of tea and coffee and we knew her name was Mary. Widowed two months, she was enroute home from a clinic with a prescription she didn't want to fill: Get rid of her husband's clothes and all his pictures, take off her rings and start a new life.

"Makes you glad for what you have, doesn't it?" Pat asked as we called our husbands for the third time. Both advised us to stay another night.

"Is there a reason for this?" I asked, and Pat said she thought so, but she didn't know what it was.

I took another round of cold medicine and settled in for a long nap. "I guess the reason we're here is because of my cold," I said, and she laughed as she switched on television, totally ignoring the article she'd planned to write.

Mary joined us for dinner. "You know, there's a reason for our being snowed in," she said.

"How'd you happen to stop here instead of across the road?" Pat asked.

"I don't know," Mary said. "But there has to be a reason."

146

Dinner ran into the evening's entertainment. We laughed so much during the first show we stayed for the second. "This is the first time I've laughed since my husband died," Mary said.

Pat nodded. "That's the reason you stopped."

By morning, the roads were cleared. Frost clung to the trees like spun sugar and the snow glistened in the sun as we parted, planning to get together again, two friends made three by the storm.

There was a reason for all that, I thought as I drove home, giving thanks for the family that waited for me and praying that Mary's life would change. My cold was decidedly better, the day was beautiful, traffic flowed easily. Everything that had happened seemed like a dream, a dream with a reason.

And then I learned it had not snowed at home.

"Hi, Snow Bunny," Loren greeted me, and I knew there was a reason for his smile. He was remembering a day he'd been grounded by fog in Ohio and I'd been somewhat less good-natured about the changes his absence had made in my plans. So that was the reason, I thought as I returned his greeting. I liked his way better.

Todd only grinned as he rushed off to a project, and Doug said, "See you made it home."

"Gee," I said.

Sensing my dejection, he said, "I missed you, Mom." He pulled up his pants leg and showed me the reason. He was out of matching socks.

Mother's Night Out

When your life settles into a drab month-in-month-out routine of getting up, going to work, going home, cooking, cleaning and scrubbing, and the most exciting thing that happened all week was the unexpected matching of a pair of

147

socks in your steadily growing odd-sock pile, and the most fun thing you can recommend to your children is making a batch of popcorn, it is time to do something.

Psychologists and other advice-givers suggest a mother's night out to get away from home and kids and develop a new outlook on life.

After a month of not matching a single sock, even the excitement of popcorn couldn't break that is-this-all-there-is-to-life feeling, and it was apparent the time had come. I joined three other mothers for dinner at a Japanese restaurant. We would forget homework and baskets of mateless socks for one night.

We were seated with a couple from Iowa, kindred spirits, free, they said, for a weekend without children. And wasn't it true, they asked, that four and six-year-olds were the worst? We debated the issue, each hating to agree another age could be more difficult than that of our own children. Clearly, our night out was not off to a good start.

Only the arrival of our colorful waiter ended the discussion. Dressed in native Japanese fashion, a yellow chef's hat and matching scarf completing his ensemble, he held us spellbound as he prepared the meal in the center of our table, which contained a gas burner. With a flourish he tossed out shrimp and cut off the tails, halved the rest, cooked them lightly and placed them in heated bowls. Just like me sorting socks, I thought, here a black one, there a blue one. If only I could do my housework with that much grace. . . . I pushed the thoughts from my mind, dimly aware that onions, bamboo shoots, bean sprouts, mushrooms and steak had followed. This was called getting away from it all, not thinking about home all the time.

I clutched my chopsticks and hoped no one was watching. The first bite was a success, and I applauded myself. But laughter told me I'd really failed. "You've got your chopsticks upside down," a friend whispered. I never got another bite after I turned them around, but the concentration pushed away thoughts of sorting socks until I finally asked for a fork. The rice tasted better with a fork and, while it made me think of bowls of popcorn, I tried to keep from wondering what the boys were doing for excitement while their mother took her night out.

Actually, the night out changed our lives. At least it added color. I brought each boy a set of chopsticks and they provided their own excitement by making popcorn almost every night because it was the only thing they could pick up with their chopsticks. The sight brightened many a night of trying to match socks. In fact, on my first attempt after our night out, I matched five pairs, breaking my previous record and giving cause to believe there is something to be said for occasionally following a psychologist's advice.

Roughing It

In order to give opposing sides equal time, it must be reported mothers are not the only people who sometimes need a night out.

"How about us?" the boys asked when they read the previous story. "Have you forgotten the night we went out?"

I hadn't forgotten.

Roughing it was what they called the night away from the family table. Plans to camp overnight were squelched by threats of rain, and it was with some reluctance they finally agreed their night out would be supper only, to be eaten in a lean-to they had built in the woods.

They planned a simple menu, one that gave me few problems. I filled our vintage camping utensils with beans and two kinds of hot dogs, all carefully wrapped in foil to stay hot, and a thermos of hot chocolate. Cookies and potato chips went into a paper bag with carrots, apples and napkins.

"Your food's ready," I called. They reluctantly pried themselves away from a rerun of "Gilligan's Island" and loaded their supplies in a trailer behind the tractor and chugged to the woods.

Loren and I were barely finished with our own supper, the quietest one we could remember in years, when they returned.

"How was the chocolate?"

"Hot."

"The hot dogs?"

"Good."

"Did you have fun?"

"Sure. We made it back in time for 'Gunsmoke,' didn't we?" they said as they plopped their dirty pans on the clean cupboard, kicked off their shoes and headed back to the living room.

Their roughing-it night out had taken exactly one hour.

But they had learned why their father occasionally goes flying by himself and why their mother sometimes takes a night out or goes to workshops: Our love for each other is not diminished by these excursions. Rather, it is restored, rejuvenated. These times away fill a need Jesus must have felt when he went off by himself to pray — the need to get things into a new perspective, with ourselves, with God and with each other.

CHAPTER SEVENTEEN

Footprints in the Wind

Bleach Bottles and Lib

I was thirty-seven years old before anyone told me I did not have the best of two worlds, that my only world was the one alloted me as Woman and that it was all bad. I did not like what I heard.

"You witch!" I wanted to shout. "You crazy, dumb witch!"

The speaker was Kate, a member of a newly organized women's liberation group. The more she talked, the angrier I became. And, in spite of myself, intrigued.

"I have no last name," she said. "My father gave me one and my husband gave me another; I've never had one of my own." Dressed in tattered jeans, a too-tight jersey that left no doubt her bra had joined her make-up in the trash barrel, dirty feet stuffed into suede clogs, she said, "If a woman breaks a barrier, you know her measurements. If a man does, you never know his."

It was 1971. Betty Friedan had been telling us for years that we needed to be liberated, but Kate was the first self-proclaimed "libber" I had seen. I agreed when she said, "I'm looking forward to the time a mediocre woman gets the same pay as a mediocre man," but I was unprepared for her next angry protest. "Why should our husbands' paychecks be made out to them? We worked for that money

151

too. Every check my husband gets has both our names on it."

"Does your check have his name on it, too?" someone asked. Kate ignored the question.

"What is important?" another voice called.

"Love," Kate said. "My husband is home baking bread while I'm speaking; I can put oil in the car if I have to. Love takes care of things."

"So your husband is home baking bread," I thought. "What does that prove? Is this another victory you've won?" But I remembered Loren was sitting with the boys so I could have a day off, and I said nothing. It didn't matter. One of my more vocal colleagues was already on her feet. She did a turn and curtsy to demonstrate the capabilities of latex and said, "Frankly, I like wearing a bra. I don't want to look or feel like a cow. I am a woman. And I like make-up and dresses and flowers and perfume."

"If you want to keep on clinging to a sexist urge to look like a Barbie doll, good for you," Kate said.

"Who washes the dishes in your house?" someone asked.

"What do you mean, who washes the dishes?" Kate snapped.

"I mean there are things that have to be done around the house and dishes are among them. Who does them?"

"My husband and I love each other."

"Does this answer the question? Do the dishes get washed?"

"Certainly, this answers the question. My husband and I love each other. That's enough. It's not important who washes the dishes."

By now the discussion had become a pitched battle between Kate and several dozen journalists, women whose combined talents had produced books, copy for newspapers and magazines, the wire services, radio and television. Most had husbands, homes and children and had worked

152

hard to establish their own best of two worlds lifestyles. Many of the older members could remember lobbying for women's right to vote. This talk of "liberation" was disquieting.

Somehow, the discussion changed from woman's traditional role as homemaker, babysitter and chauffeur to the "society pages." "They are horrid, anachronisms that should be discarded," Kate snorted.

"I never read them," a guest said defensively.

"Don't be such a snob," a woman's editor snapped. "You might be surprised at what you find there."

She would have said more, but her words were cut short by a gentle, timid voice from the back of the room. "Leave them as they are, but please don't give us any more 'Fifteen Things To Make Out Of Bleach Bottles.' "

Everyone stopped talking and looked for the speaker. Not finding her, they applauded. Where there had been disagreement, there was unity: Women deserved better than that.

I came away from the meeting with mixed feelings. I cherished the traditional values on which I'd been reared, and I liked the multi-roles in which I had been cast—wife, mother, daughter, writer, editor, homemaker, church member, community worker. It didn't matter in what order they were listed or if they were scrambled, they were my life. But was I missing something? Were my readers missing something?

I ran a filler about a woman who won a transcontinental air race. No comment.

"How about it?" I asked. "Which you do want—bleach bottles or liberation?" For good measure, I threw in forty-eight uses for bleach bottles.

The Bottles Have It

"Which do you want?" I had asked. "Do you think in terms

153

of bleach bottles or accomplishments or a mixture of both? Be sure to let me know."

They did.

Women's Lib took a beating, not only from readers who were "just housewives"—an anachronism that should be weighted in a bleach bottle full of cement and put into orbit—but from career women, women whose lives had been anything but safe and women who hadn't done their own housework since the local cleaning service opened.

"It's a Communist plot," said one.

"A good woman inspires a man; a brilliant woman interests him; a beautiful woman fascinates him; and a sympathetic woman gets him," another quoted from an anonymous source. She didn't say what happened to a liberated woman.

"My opinions aren't even quotable, let alone printable," said another. "It's a horrid topic."

"You wanted to know if we wanted bleach bottle projects or accomplishments," a reader wrote. "I'd rather accomplish something with bleach bottles."

I hadn't anticipated the backlash nor had I anticipated being invited to represent the state's weeklies at a workshop. The topic? "Liberating the Women's Pages."

How could I discuss liberating women's pages? I didn't know if they needed liberating. Liberated from what? Bleach bottles?

I gulped when I saw the speaker who was to precede me, an editor with an armload of awards and an easily recognizable by-line. Perhaps I can get ideas from her that would apply to a weekly, I thought as I listened carefully. "Concentrate on people," she said. "Concentrate on what they are doing that is good. Bad, too, if you have to, but don't harp on the same old subjects. You report one abortion, you've done them all."

"We don't use abortion stories," I said when it was my

turn to speak. "Our readers know who is having them; there's no need to sensationalize." I went on to describe our readers as liberated women who could drive tractors, milk cows, midwife pregnant sows and coach Little League teams with the same skill they used in creating dresses to wear when they poured tea for the governor's wife. "Our women don't need liberating and neither do our women's pages," I said. "We're all liberated where I come from."

The audience roared its approval. I should have remembered the old adage that compliments are like perfume — meant to be inhaled, not swallowed — but I swallowed quite a few before I heard a voice hiss my name. "You thought you were amusing, but you weren't." The speaker was the woman's editor of a metropolitan daily. "Have you ever been denied credit because you were a divorced woman? Have you ever had trouble finding a decent apartment because you had no husband and weren't considered a good risk? Have you ever been discriminated against?" I had to admit I had felt little discrimination. "Well, I have," she said, "and it's not a good feeling. You and your readers should remember there's more to being 'liberated' than helping sows farrow. There are such things as equal rights, too."

"I believe in equal pay for equal work," I said defensively.

"That's just a start," she replied. "There's a whole different world out there for women. Go back and see what else your women are doing besides milking cows."

Our conversation was cut short by another workshop, but her remarks haunted me. I've got the best of two worlds, maybe three, I argued to myself. All I really need to make my life complete is a little free time.

But the questions I had heard raised in the past weeks nagged me. What were we missing? I re-evaluated our paper, by then the combination of our first weekly and one we had purchased two years later, and found the answer all of us on the panel had missed—even having a woman's page was discrimination.

I threw away the woman's and farm page headings, some of the canned fillers and found a lot of space, mostly on the center pages. A centerfold? Our answer to Playboy and Cosmopolitan? No. I figured a nude was like an abortion, you'd done one, you'd done them all. This would be different.

Armed with a camera, I set off like Diogenes with his lantern, questing not an honest man but men and women who were accomplishing something with or without bleach bottles. The result was a crazy quilt of highly talented people, each with very real hopes and fears for themselves and for the future.

I found, as I predicted, women who were midwifing sows, milking cows and driving tractors, but I found, too, women running for Congress, doing macramé, rope sculpture, teaching painting and weaving, attending Bible classes and wing riding. Women who were business executives and women who were picking up broken pieces of their lives by teaching remedial reading, studying the crafts of eggery, ceramics and straw, or working in nursing homes. I found men who loved housework, a boy who won the 4-H dress revue with the apron he made, a man who created exquisite lamps and another who raised bees and gave recipes to his honey customers. And there were others, too, like the one-armed aerobatic pilot, the paraplegic who built toys that worked, the woodworkers and caners and the men who played polo with brooms and gave the admission fees to charity.

It was an asinine question, one that shouldn't have been asked, but I persisted. "Are you liberated?" I never found anyone who was or who wanted to be. "That's okay for some people, I guess, but not me," a woman said as she dismantled the engine of her airplane, corrected the problem and re-

156

assembled it. "You're as liberated as you let yourself be," said the executive of a large lumber company as she surveyed the firm's mechanized yard and recalled her early days in the woods. "Liberated from what?" a reporter asked as she rushed to conduct a seminar on liberating newspapers. "I don't have time to be liberated," a farm wife said as she finished her school bus route and prepared to help her husband pick corn. For others, the mothers of illegitimate children, the mothers whose children were coming too fast, whose men no longer loved them or never had, liberation was a vague thing—a nice goal, but one they would forget if they could find love.

The people I interviewed reinforced my glib statement that our readers didn't need liberating, but, instead of being reassured, I was depressed. It's not surprising that this was the time stress took its toll, because I was confused about who I was, where I was going and where I had been. "Isn't there more to life than this?" I asked as I readied pages for the printer. At the same time I reminded myself that the offset process had liberated me from the hot metal we once used, the seventy-five pound forms of type I'd moved until time to deliver Doug and resumed moving within two weeks after his birth. And I thought of Mary Katherine Goddard and the print shop in which she printed the Declaration of Independence two hundred years ago and shuddered that it had taken almost that long for women to get the right to vote.

And I looked at the militant feminists, women far more vocal than Kate, and found nothing I liked—no sense of humor, no willingness to give a little, to really let go and love. Their lives were as sterile as a bottle of bleach, but there would be no fifteen different things to do with them—or forty-eight or one hundred—because they didn't seem to know what they wanted.

And I attended other workshops and got conflicting ideas.

157

"You simply can't treat all your brides as equals, because they aren't," an editor said—the same one who had said there was more to liberation than farrowing sows and milking cows. "But we think all our brides are important," I protested. "That doesn't work," she said. "You can't run the same sized picture for the garbage collector's daughter that you do for the banker's daughter."

"We do," I said quietly, wishing I were home sorting ink and manure stains, or watching the boys eat popcorn with chopsticks, or flying with Loren.

"What did you learn at your meeting?" they asked when I came home.

"It's a crazy time to be a woman," I replied.

"I could've told you that," Doug said as he carried food to the table Todd had set and called their father who greeted me with a kiss and the decency to say nothing.

Footprints in the Wind and Post-Natal Drip

> The wind blows wherever it chooses, and you hear the sound of it, but you do not know where it comes from or where it goes. —John 3:8

The years have flown since Kate and her fellow women rocked our lives. The war in Vietnam has ended, but peace is still as elusive as a cure for cancer. Life and death and the quest for equality, or even a definition of it, go on.

In the meantime, each of us casts myriad footprints in the wind as we race from being the person we were six years ago to the one we will be six years from now. Our spiritual rebirth may be in the past, but the wet behind our ears seems to be still drying.

My family's footprints tend to be caked with mud and ink;

158

like everyone else our Christian life has been wet with doubts and fears. Are we rearing our family as we should? Is this the right profession? What will we leave for our children? And self-pity. It's not fair that we never have vacations, that our days and nights often run into each other. We protest, even as we give thanks for the privilege of pursuing the best of our two lives—secular and Christian, urban and rural—and that balance hasn't come easily.

But we see signs of other footprints, some leaving traces of blood, oppression, greed, hunger and fear, and we drop our heads in shame for being so self-centered and thank God for the mud and ink.

Like the post-natal imperfections, the quest for equality will continue until we meet again in heaven where, Galatians tells us, there is neither Jew nor Greek, neither bond nor free, neither male nor female; "for you are all one in Christ Jesus." In the meantime, the spiritual moisture can sometimes be swabbed away temporarily by the scented tissues our television hucksters promote, but the lack of what should be the inalienable right of everyone cannot be eradicated with a quick swipe by a mop-riding fairy. Nor can it be assuaged by a change of language to "herstory," "chairperson" or "home management specialist."

It's going to take a turning to God, a constant acknowledgment of what his love for us as manifested in his Son really means. And there will be no room for closet Christians as we all join in the search for the way he would have us travel, the way in which rich men and poor men—and women—are treated equally in his sight.

It's taken me all these years to realize how alike Kate and I were in spite of our differences, but since she didn't tell us her last name, I have no idea how to find her to tell her. Like a million footprints, she is lost in the wind, but her central theme is as valid today as it was then or when Loren and I decided to pursue our new birth lifestyle: Love is the most important thing.

Like equality, love can't be legislated; it has to be freely given and carefully nourished. If it isn't, the newborn babe will stay wet behind the ears and never grow up to be the mature person Christ wants us to become.

The End